START THE CLOCK AND CUE THE BAND **A LIFE IN TELEVISION**

Margaret

For the old times —
and the new —
Love
David Penrose

JUNE 2016.

For my two daughters,
Melanie Justine and Naomi Ruth,
who I love unreservedly as I do my grandchildren,
Fraser, Daisy and Pippa

START THE CLOCK
AND CUE THE BAND # A LIFE IN
TELEVISION

David Lloyd

Cover design: Y Lolfa
Cover photograph: David Lloyd with Colin Pickford

ISBN: 978 1 78461 067 8

Published and printed in Wales
on paper from well-maintained forests by
Y Lolfa Cyf., Talybont, Ceredigion SY24 5HE
website www.ylolfa.com
e-mail ylolfa@ylolfa.com
tel 01970 832 304
fax 832 782

Contents

Preface

Chance is part of reality.
We are continually shaped by the forces of coincidence.
The unexpected occurs with almost numbing regularity.

Paul Auster

MY FATHER'S EXPECTATIONS for me were far removed from what I actually became. Although he recognised that hard work was the only way to achieve, he was largely influenced by the principles of the managerial classes around him, namely, scholarly achievement through academic commitment. My failure to pass that awful 11-plus examination must have come as a bitter blow, although my absenteeism from school because of ill-health would have given him forewarning of my slow development. I was also a 'war baby' and prone to the trauma of bombing raids which must have been detrimental for any child. However, parental love and guidance was never in short supply and I soldiered forth.

The cinema, the theatre, radio and the re-emergence of television in those post-war years played a significant part in my development, but would have been viewed as educationally valueless in deepest, darkest rural Wales, although schools did regimentally march their pupils to the local fleapit to watch Shakespeare's *Julius Caesar*, the Coronation, and the conquest of Everest.

Already I was beginning to find my path, but the struggle and the twists and turns ahead lay in wait and I had little chance to avoid them, other than battle through the unexpected with a resilience that came from somewhere deep down.

To those readers far removed from my world, every recorded television programme had to be identified with a clock and cueing the band or something or someone was essential if there was to be a programme.

I hope my life story, complete with its vibrancy, its laughter and heartache, will tell you something of me and of an industry to which I felt unfailingly attached – an industry that in the 1950s and in the years that followed changed our everyday lives forever.

David Lloyd

Foreword

WHAT A PRIVILEGE to be invited to write this foreword to a book by my good friend and fellow Aberystwythian, David Lloyd. We have so much in common. We have the sound of the sea crashing on the Cardigan Bay rocks ringing in our ears. We both witnessed the exciting media developments in our capital city, Cardiff in the 1960s, '70s and '80s when we both paid homage to that great broadcaster, Wynford Vaughan-Thomas, one of the founders of Harlech Television, later to become HTV.

In this book David has recorded the story of his youth, his teenage years and subsequent career. After his drama college training, achieving his ambition in 1963 to work in the media was going to take perseverance and sacrifice on a scale his family could not have imagined. In a distinctive and compelling narrative, David recalls the trials and tribulations of finding work in an overcrowded profession, namely the theatre, and later battling to prove his worth in the world of television that was already saturated with young creative people seeking golden careers. He relates the endless search for work, the humiliation of the dole queue, and finding a TV mogul somewhere who would look sympathetically on a young man and give him that lucky break.

This 'roller coaster' autobiography will take you from Aberystwyth to London, from Norwich to Aberdeen, from Cardiff to Europe, America, Israel, Africa and Japan. From Los Angeles to Merthyr Tydfil and all corners of Wales, before returning to the peace and tranquillity of his native Ceredigion.

This story, full of pathos and humour, is a fascinating read. It's the story of the making of David Lloyd, the eminent television director and producer: a man much respected and admired in broadcasting circles in Wales. *Start the Clock and Cue the Band – A Life in Television* is an irresistible read – it's magic!

David Meredith
Former Head of Press and Public Relations,
HTV and S4C Television

Acknowledgements

START THE CLOCK and Cue the Band – A Life in Television was two years in the writing and over 40 years in the making. Many friends assisted me with stories and pictures from a time when Independent Television was excitingly different from anything else on television in this country. I thank you all, but the book is not just about television but about the tapestry of a life in which all my contributors played such a significant role.

Firstly, I thank David Meredith, a highly respected Welshman who's roots, like mine, are based in Aberystwyth in Ceredigion. We were to rediscover our friendship years later in HTV Wales. A man of great cultural substance, his words in the Foreword give my autobiography weight and credibility. Diolch yn fawr, David.

My deepest gratitude goes to Mair Stanleigh, a friend of mine for many years and an excellent teacher of the English language. Now in her ninth decade, she would read my chapters with meticulous care and hand them back to me if none of it made sense. Our discussions went on long into the night.

There are others who deserve a mention.

My editor and publisher, namely Eirian Jones and Lefi Gruffudd, both respectively of Y Lolfa deserve medals for seeing it as a publishable book.

Thank you to Jean and Alan Sutton, my sister and brother-in-law; Richard Martin Lloyd, my brother; and Richard and Bethan Lewis, my cousin and his wife, for all their support and encouragement.

Huw Davies (*quondam* Chief Executive, HTV Wales) gave me permission to quote him in the final chapter. Don Llewellyn (friend, producer and author) checked out the inevitable errors whilst the final proof reading was kindly undertaken by Pamela Ellis and Rose Billington of Aberystwyth. Thank you one and all.

My Scottish friends and ex-colleagues in the Midlands and in Scotland offered me pictures and information that I had long forgotten. Thank you to Eileen Doris Bremner for her stories, Douglas Kynoch for the Doric, Fiona Kennedy, Hector and Eva Stewart, James and Jay Spankie, Tim Spring, Graham and Allain McLeish, and Eddie and Sheena Joffe – all offered me genuine support. My thanks also to Dr Meredydd Evans and Keith and Barbara Webster.

I am grateful to the two training colleges featured in the book for giving me their permission to write about my time in their early days: The Rose Bruford College of Theatre and Performance and The Royal Welsh College of Music and Drama – The National Conservatoire of Wales, respectively.

Support material, permission and cooperation has not been in short supply from BBC Wales and ITV Wales in Cardiff and ITV Anglia in Norwich. My gratitude to these organisations.

Five ladies allowed me to use pictures of their late husbands, all of whom touched my life at different times. Fiona Palmer, with a picture of my early voice tutor, Peter; Sian Morris, for a picture of Geraint; Elinor Elias Jones, for her picture of Peter; Catrin Gerallt, for allowing me to include a picture of Emyr Daniel; and Jane Franchi in Aberdeen for the pictures of Alan.

Professor Yahnke of the University of Minnesota gave me his permission to use his quote on the film star Marlon Brando and thanks also to The Society of Authors as the literary representative of the Estate of John Masefield, and to W. H. Masefield. Special thanks to Dr John Maynard for quoting him in Chapter Two. Many friends helped me with my trip down memory lane and allowed me use of their names and stories. They are: Nicola Heywood-Thomas, Tweli Griffiths, Paul Starling, Mike Roberts, Russell Isaac, Sara Jones, Arfon Haines Davies, Bob Symonds, Alan Rustad, Rosemary Scadden,

Margaret Pritchard, Dusashen, Elinor Jones, Roger Richards, Mike Lloyd-Williams, Stuart Leyshon, Ron Lewis and Michael Roberts.

My thanks to Faber and Faber for their permission to use Paul Auster's quote from *Moon Palace* in this book's Preface and special thanks go to the National Library of Wales for all their research in finding pictures from the old HTV Wales archive. I make special mention of William Troughton and Simon Evans in the library and Phil Henfrey and Owain Meredith at ITV Wales. Finally my gratitude to Sheila Johnson for the back cover photograph and Simon Johnson (no relation) for the front cover picture.

Mention must be made of one other woman and that is Annette, my former wife, who is mentioned more than once throughout the book. She, amongst all family and domestic upheaval, unflinchingly and unselfishly, gave me two wonderful daughters and the space and latitude to develop my career. Thank you, Annette.

David Lloyd
December 2014

1

Nervous Beginnings

THERE WAS BLOOD on the sheets when I woke that morning; my mother stripped the bed and washed the lot. She was as used to the task as I was to scratching. The skin on my hands, on my feet and behind my knees was shredded and blood oozed out of cuts that stiffened my fingers for weeks as the sore and chapped skin tried to regenerate itself. I had carried the burden of eczema and asthma bravely for as long as I could remember but whenever something important was about to be faced in my life, the conditions worsened. Teenage years invariably bring their own problems but what lay ahead of me in one month's time resulted in a flare-up of my skin condition and gave me breathing problems. I had one month to get my hands working again. The frequent application of creams and ointments was essential, as was a supreme effort to conquer the nerves that were crippling my style, if indeed I ever had one. There was one month left and I was trying to delay every second.

***

I was born in 1940 in Aberystwyth on the west Wales coast to the sound of surf breaking over sand and pebble, and mountain breezes in the tall, sturdy beech trees that flanked our back garden. Such an idyllic setting was soon to be swapped for the city streets of Cardiff, for we were at war with an enemy I was too young to comprehend. My father's national service was with the RAF ground crew in St Athan and I resided with my mother and grandmother in the Splott area of Cardiff.

During the air raids we sat crouched in a Morrison shelter which also served as the kitchen table. It was a hefty piece of furniture, made from iron with mesh sides to it. It was there I learned that the world was a troublesome place and that the threatening drone of German aeroplanes over our city every night was not something to be relished. It meant being woken up, taken down to a freezing kitchen, thrust into the shelter with my grandparents, and praying the bombs would not get any closer. The wail of a siren frightens me, even today. I could remember, years later, my father saying that during the three-night blitz on Swansea, he could see the glow from the fires in the night sky from Aberystwyth. I was relieved when the sirens stopped and we all celebrated Victory in Europe Day in a street party and sat around a bonfire where the old water tank had stood down in Moorland Road. My collection of shrapnel was impressive but carrying a gas mask to school and being made to wear it was something I deplored. My Dad was demobbed after the war and in 1945 my sister was born and later that year we returned to the sun, the sea and the scenery of Aberystwyth.

***

Our father was born in 1905 and he was, without doubt, a good man – helpful to others, caring to us kids and a strong support to my mother. Hewn from the hills of Cardiganshire, he was born in Devil's Bridge and was one of ten children who were all fluent in the Welsh language. Family records on his side point to us originating from Dumfries in Scotland. We walked, or so the story goes, from there in the 17th century, with our animals but did not settle until we reached the Nant-y-Moch, Ponterwyd area of Cardiganshire. My father felt close to his place of birth and whenever relatives from further afield called on us, he would insist on showing them the scenic view across the Rheidol valley from the top road to Devil's Bridge.

Our Dad did more for tourism in Cardiganshire than anyone would believe.

My mother, nine years younger than my father, was born in Cardiff, although her maiden name of McCreadie also suggests Scottish ancestry. She was one of two other siblings – a brother, and a sister, Joyce, who died of meningitis at a young age. Mum's occupation was secretarial and she would cycle down to Cardiff docks each day, sometimes getting the wheels of her bike caught in the tramlines that zigzagged the city's roads. One day she took a trip to Aberystwyth and was introduced to my father: the rest is history.

Such was the seriousness of my many health problems that my Dad sprang into action. He had read of a hypnotist in Great Yarmouth who could do great things for people with eczema. He decided we should go to see the man. Great Yarmouth is some distance from Aberystwyth and, in the 1950s, it seemed even further. The main aim of the visit was to eradicate my allergy to nuts and fish – a blight on my life from infancy.

With the first stage of the journey ending in Birmingham, we booked in at a guest house and spotted a room packed full with residents watching the first television set I had ever seen. I was speechless. What on earth was it? Curiosity and a basic understanding of how a cinema worked encouraged me to look for a projector. How was that small, glowing, black and white, fuzzy picture being beamed onto that tiny box in the corner? I looked around and could see nothing but the faces of strangers in the room. The picture revealed the fact we were in a London taxi cab, parked outside a glitzy West End theatre. A uniformed gentleman opened the taxi door and we were invited to step inside. There, to the sound of music and applause, Maurice Chevalier stepped out onto the stage and welcomed us to *In Town Tonight*. What a stunning invention for a small boy to witness. I should have stayed in Birmingham watching this staggering piece of technology. Instead, it was on to Great Yarmouth to meet the hypnotist my father could not stop talking about.

"You will now feel sleepy, David, and your eyelids are getting heavier."

I was standing to attention, looking at this doctor between the eyes and thinking of that television back in Birmingham. My father was sitting in the corner of the room looking impressed. The good doctor continued.

"So heavy, so sleepy, let yourself drift, drift, drift away. I will support you into the soft chair behind you where you will lie back and relax and sleep."

Wrong, I couldn't sleep because I was thinking of that television in Birmingham! I will keep my eyes closed and hope for the best.

"Is he really asleep?" asked my father from the corner of the room.

"Oh yes," replied the doctor. "Soundly asleep but he can hear every word I utter."

I could hear my father reaching for his cheque book. The doctor must be joking. I am wide awake, pretending to be asleep. Get me back to that television.

"David, you will rise from the armchair now, take the glass tumbler from my desk and place it on the telephone stand next to your chair. You will then sit back and continue to sleep. When you eventually reach home, you will discover that you can eat fish and enjoy it."

I thought to myself, when I go home I hope it's via Birmingham. The doctor clapped his hands three times and I opened my eyes.

"Can you see anything strange about this room David?" It has no television I thought to myself. "Yes, yes," I replied. "The glass tumbler has moved from your desk and it's now on that little telephone table."

My father was beside himself with excitement; his pen poised over his cheque book.

When we arrived home I rushed into the house and asked my mother for fish and chips for lunch. She willingly obliged, after which I rushed upstairs and was unutterably ill whilst my

father, downstairs, was counting the cost. Another treatment
gone... but I did like that television.

**

My teachers in school had spotted my shyness when facing
others and used it to their advantage. Being called out to face
the class in primary school brought torment and anxiety. I was
declared a dunce in arithmetic and English and standing in the
corner facing the wall would warn others of similar ineptitude
to start learning fast or they would face the same embarrassing
punishment. If in arithmetic I was a failure, in poetry I excelled
and astounded my English teacher one day by standing in front
of the class and reciting, off by heart, Hilaire Belloc's 'Matilda'.
There was silence when I finished it. The class of kids and my
teacher had witnessed something out of character and all sat in
silent admiration. Was this a flash in the pan or had something
uncorked itself in my development? My memory, I discovered,
was something that was going to serve me well in the years to
come.

Life was not all doom and gloom. The sun shone for seven
days a week during our summer holidays. It never rained from
what I can remember. There were long days of sunshine to play
endlessly in the meadows and woods surrounding my home.
As young lads, we raided orchards and helped ourselves to as
much fruit as our grey, short trouser-pockets could hold. With
my buddies I dammed streams, built dens in hedges and barns
and ran riot through fields of sheep. When it was time for bed,
mother would stand on the doorstep and ring a little brass bell.
The other mothers would do the same, and distinguishing the
different bells was never a problem no matter how far away we
were, but every night the cry would go up, "Please mum... only
five minutes more."

My mother and her brother (my Uncle Alex) were responsible
for encouraging my love of theatre and cinema. They both
adored live stage shows and they both loved visiting the cinema;

being city people they probably had easy access to it, unlike my father who was from rural Wales and not used to the noise, the clatter and bright lights of the city. He was born during the time of the great religious revival in Wales when the world of film was in its infancy and when some people saw more harm than good coming from this new-fangled invention. He was not entirely happy with me going to the cinema and, in David Berry's book, *Wales and Cinema – the First Hundred Years*, Will Aaron, a highly respected Aberystwyth-born film maker is quoted as saying, "… film stank slightly of gin and the sweat of the fairground." My father, seeing me with my nose pressed to the displays outside the cinema, informed me that they made it all in bits and I would be disappointed at the process. However, I was brought up in the 1940s, when the American and British film industries were at their peak and, when my father allowed it, I was an eager patron of the town's three cinemas and the full thrust of the silver screen's publicity machine.

***

In my early teenage years, I had three reasons for going to Pontrhydyfen in south Wales for my holidays. My grandmother lived there, Richard Burton had come from there, and I wanted to meet Carol again. The need to walk with a girlfriend was more of an urge than a need, and Carol had captured my attention. She lived down by the railway line that carried the coal trains to the blast furnaces in Port Talbot. She had that Welsh, olive complexion, dark hair and a smile that weakened me to my knees. I chased her relentlessly and my young sister insisted on following us everywhere. Something was burning a hole in my soul for love and Carol in her white ankle socks, brown patent sandals and plaid skirt was either beating a hasty retreat or encouraging me to do the chasing. I could never quite work out which. We kissed down by the river under that enormous viaduct that spans the village. I often wondered what happened to her, and years later a colleague from my place of work informed me that he too came from the same village and that they sang in the same choir. He brought in a photograph of the choir and, for old times' sake, I rang her and we laughed and talked about the good old days. The conversation, although friendly enough, reminded me of the concluding chapter of a romantic novel. We had both changed and life had moved on. We had become adults and those raw emotions of youth had evaporated like the melting snow on the coal tips surrounding the village.

My grandmother's house was split by a narrow road. The small scullery with its back garden and the living room with its open fire, china dogs and brass kettles was on one side of the road, and the two bedrooms and the 'best room' with paper flowers and family Bible was on the other. You would see neighbours clutching their oil lamps and crossing the road to go to bed. What was good about all this was my grandmother knew Hilda, Richard Burton's sister. I longed to meet this great film star but he was never at home, but Hilda, God bless her, did get me his autograph to which he added his photograph. I treasure it to this day.

***

I well remember our first television coming into the house. With a small black and white picture it sat in the living room taking up premium space, with all of us sitting watching the Test Card until the start of programmes at teatime. All the furniture needed rearranging in the room to watch this amazing piece of miniature cinema. I felt the same excitement as I had felt in Birmingham all those years ago and now family life would never be the same again. Miss Jones, an elderly lady from up the road, joined us every Sunday to watch *Dr Finlay's Casebook*. Watching Gilbert Harding on *What's My Line* on a Sunday night and Eamonn Andrews in *This is your Life* on Monday evening brought a ritualistic, communal sitting-down experience that we had not shared for some time. We might have missed the Coronation, the conquest of Everest and the Festival of Britain but bought the television set in time for Richard Dimbleby's April Fool's trick about the spaghetti harvest on *Panorama* – which was very much a spoof yarn telling us about how spaghetti grew on bushes in Italy and was harvested once a year. It fooled the country but I don't think my family had ever seen or tasted spaghetti, so it took some time for the story to penetrate.

***

The month was up. My skin was mildly better although the backs of my knees were still showing red. The problem was the nerves. I could not stop shaking and the nerves usually made me scratch my skin mercilessly. The occasion was the boy scout enrolment ceremony in our church hall. I wore my uniform bravely and I looked the part but I was worried about the lines I would have to recite to my scout master, to the troop and to the watching crowds, most of whom were parents, all waiting to hear my oath of allegiance, with stage fright taking over.

It was a complex ceremony where badges, wooden poles and handshakes were exchanged and scout laws repeated in a certain order. Even the handshake was done with the left hand while the right hand received a badge. There was a dress rehearsal and I messed it up and I knew I was going to let everyone down and be a total disaster. I worried for days and felt sick to the pit of my stomach. I could not remember the lines, my memory was non-existent. I wheezed and took a blast of my puffer – a glass inhaler with a mask for relieving the symptoms of asthma. The hall was packed to capacity. The scout master went down the line and called out each boy. I was at the end of the line, with knees visibly shaking and my mind a total blank. If the ground had opened up and swallowed me there and then, I would have been more than happy. I promise to do my duty to God and the Queen and...? Where there should have been words, there were none. I tripped and stumbled and blushed. The handshake was wrong and I had left my pole with the scout master by mistake. I quickly walked back to my line ashamed and distressed by the calamity of it all. I wanted to die. I was devastated and, to make matters worse, the scout master bade me return and repeat the whole thing all over again. My parents would feel ashamed and embarrassed and I could hear the kids sniggering behind me. I ran home that night and went straight to bed with tear-stained cheeks. Dreaming of the horrors of Hitler's Luftwaffe was preferable to thinking about the disastrous scout enrolment ceremony. My self-esteem and confidence had taken another blow and I was never going to recover.

If my guardian angel was watching over me at that point in my development, she was about to come to my rescue, for what was about to happen would change my life irrevocably.

CHAPTER 2

Treading the Boards

THE CHANGE IN my life came in the form of a Christmas gift. It was a book entitled *The Boys' Book of Magic*. I peeled off the Christmas wrapping and studied the front cover. *Secrets of conjuring explained in a way that every boy can understand.* The picture showed a young lad, dressed smartly, holding a star-spangled tin and from it he is producing a string of coloured silks. Either side of him are two small circular tables on which there are various magical props: cubes, an egg, some cones, an up-turned top hat, a glass and a pack of cards. Everyday objects. Behind the lad is a large ethereal image of a wizard dressed in a light blue gown and a conical hat on his head bearing moons and stars. He is waving a magic wand above the lad. I studied the picture and thumbed through the pages. Given to me by a kindly neighbour, this book was not put down for a month; I read every page repeatedly. I was spellbound. I was now amongst the greatest exponents of magic in the world: John Nevil Maskelyne, David Devant, Robert Houdin, and many others. My growing-up problems disappeared on the wind as I vowed to devote my future life to the art of magic. As the book stated, '... a conjurer is always a great favourite anywhere'.

Unfortunately, the thought of indulging in magic all day became even less of a reality as my father reminded me that finding a job was more important than making cigarettes disappear in front of the bedroom mirror. My parents had a strong desire to see me settled, and in those days an apprenticeship to one of the trades or to a job in a bank or an office were considered fundamental to any future career. I became one of the County Treasurer's junior clerks.

We paid the bills to all the suppliers who provided the County Council with a service, namely suppliers to schools, residential homes and road contractors. There were black telephones for outside calls and green telephones for internal; they never stopped ringing. A short while ago I walked into that same office to try and recapture those days long ago. The place is now deserted and the sounds came flooding back as did the snippets of conversation.

"Shop, David? Tea up. Who wants sugar?"

"Get me some fags, David, 20 Senior Service and ten Woodbine. Oh... and don't forget my Blue Band chocolate wafer."

"I'm going to the lavatory, David. Pass me the *Daily Sketch* please. Will be back in half an hour if anyone calls."

"You paid British Railways David, and there was a mistake in your adding up."

"Whose turn to do the Lampeter Co-op bill? David, come back here please."

"Can you go to the machine room please David and collect that invoice, but don't go chatting up the girls."

"You going to the pictures tonight David? Who with?"

"Mrs Moss from Welfare wants to talk with you David... something about a mistake in a bill... she's on the phone and not a happy lady. Chop, chop."

"Who's off this Saturday? Take your eyes off Gwyneth, David. She's married."

***

One man living in Aberystwyth had caught my attention. Walter Lewis was an accomplished amateur magician and entertainer of profound skill. He was an AA patrolman and moved on to become a controller for the Cardiganshire Ambulance Service but, to me as a young lad, his greatest accomplishments were on the stage. Moving effortlessly from the costume of Baron Dumblewit in pantomime to a suave magician in evening suit in summer concerts, to the accompaniment of his theme-tune, 'Smoke Gets in Your Eyes', Walter would appear on stage in an evening show dressed in dark suit, black cloak, top hat and a white cane. To me, he was the ultimate professional: a wizard of extraordinary ability who could produce cigarettes from the air and vanish them at will. Multiplying billiard balls, cards, silks, ropes and magic wands, Walter astounded everyone in the audience. He was my local hero and, on hearing of my interest in magic, came up to my parents' house to see me. I was spellbound by this man of mystery whose hands were quicker than our eyes, with a performance that was as relaxed as it was brilliant.

Never had anything pulled me up by my boot straps with such ferocity. My world changed overnight as I learned amazing feats of wizardry with coins, cigarettes, bits of string, sponge balls, silks, top hats and rabbits. Streamers and sweets appeared from nowhere and pound notes were burnt and restored, razor blades were eaten and swallowed. None of it came easily; I spent hours, days, and weeks, practising in front of the large mirror in my mother's bedroom: working on the manipulation of coins, cards, ribbons and bits of paper. My father groaned and wished I had given as much attention, in my school days, to my maths and English. I enlisted the help of a friend who became my accomplice and assistant. We practised the palming, the passes, the art of misdirection. I learned of the great magicians of the past and how they worked their skill and mystified millions.

After months of practising my magic, it was time to demonstrate before my family and they were astonished beyond belief. At last I had found something which eased my feelings of failure but I secretly knew that I would have to face my worst demon and that was to perform to a live audience. That would be taking the bull by the horns. The thought horrified me to the point of sickness but I knew in my heart of hearts it had to be done.

***

All community activities took place in the church hall in those days. Dances, whist drives, jumble sales, dinners, parties and stage performances. I decided that, with permission from the local vicar, I would perform on the church hall stage during an evening of music and dance. He frowned when I asked him. He knew of my poor reputation for solo public performances and questioned me several times before announcing my intent from the pulpit one Sunday morning. He announced us as: 'Mystico and Bryan his assistant.' His claim to the congregation was that my reputation for magic was unquestionable. I would mystify and baffle the brightest brains in the village. Move over television magician David Nixon! My true name was not revealed, but Mystico was sitting in the choir listening to the announcement, with a week to go and already my hands were soaked with perspiration as the stress levels began to show. I counted the days and practised my magic like a man possessed. Try as I might to delay the inevitable, the day dawned, the day of my first public performance in front of an audience. Bryan and I, alone on that stage – I could not stop shaking with nerves and scratching my skin.

An announcement was made and chairs were placed in rows as people gathered together excitedly to watch the evening's entertainment. The place was packed from front to back and the crescendo of noise was enough to lift the roof. Everyone had gathered to see this man of magic; no one actually knew who he was but everyone was waiting in great anticipation. With the curtains drawn across the stage, Bryan and I took our place centre stage alongside my trestle table covered in magical props. I felt sick and told Bryan so. What on earth had possessed me to take on this performance? This was not for me, I was not really a magician. I was teenager with bad skin and a wheezy chest who fell at every obstacle and failed every examination. The noise from the floor in front of the curtain was reaching crescendo levels. I felt like death and I wished I was far away from all this. Dressed in a tweed suit and black cloak with a Victorian top hat, what was I trying to prove? Walter Lewis would have been so much better. Everything was in place. My pockets bulged with various devices: coloured silks were in place and plastic eggs cleverly concealed. There were thimbles, the newspaper and liquid trick, the production box with all the streamers hidden away from inquisitive eyes, the collapsible wand, the paper flowers and the floating silver ball. Everything was perfectly placed. I wished I were dead.

The vicar clapped his hands and the hall fell silent. I could feel my knees knocking and my body trembled.

"Tonight we are pleased to welcome the magician, Mystico, and his assistant. Be prepared to be entertained. Ladies and gentlemen, give them a warm welcome. Mystico, and his assistant."

There was applause, the hall lights dimmed and the curtain swished across to reveal a sea of blackness. The applause intensified and my name was whispered across the hall. We bowed and there was silence. Where was my voice? I couldn't find my voice. I stood like a statue glued to the stage. For my friends and neighbours this would be confirmation that I was, indeed, a fool of the first order. My whole body was trembling.

We went into our first routine, my voice finding itself from somewhere, but it had developed a warble and was very weak. My lips were as dry as baked earth but, slowly and imperceptibly, my performance improved as I concentrated on my presentation and less on my nerves. I was gaining in strength. The applause was good and the crowd clapped out of kindness, but there was a visible improvement. Some lads sniggered in the front row, but now it was my turn. A ribbon changed into an egg and a cigarette appeared from midair. A green silk became a red silk and soon there was laughter as a member of the audience lent me a pound note to burn. The smouldering ash in the ashtray brought a tense silence but the pound note was discovered in a lemon which produced a gasp from the audience and a huge burst of applause. Milk disappeared into a newspaper and reappeared from a child's elbow. I was talking as fast as a machine gun, time to slow down. The egg-bag trick was a great success and my confidence was growing. Bryan was wonderful as my assistant and did all the right things at the right time. The audience and the wise-crackers in the front row looked on with astonishment as one billiard ball became five billiard balls in my hand. A pin pierced a balloon without it bursting and the silver ball took on a life of its own. My words were precise and the business of standing on the stage felt good. I was in command and the audience were easily misdirected. My months of practise were showing results and I teased the audience, imploring them to watch my empty hands as I produced a bunch of colourful paper flowers from a top hat. Silence and concern, mixed with sudden astonishment, as I produced five, deadly sharp razor blades from my mouth, all hanging from a length of cotton. We received rapturous applause from the hall. And finally, my pièce de résistance: the empty Chinese production box from which I produced sweets, silks and streamers. More applause as we took our final bow and the curtains closed. I felt as weak as a kitten and Bryan looked equally drained. People came up to us with awe across their faces and I felt as if I had undergone a re-birth.

I do believe my parents were genuinely pleased with my performance that night: not because it was going to further my education in any way but they could see it was a battle won. The whole experience had given me a new-found confidence and a sense of purpose which could only help in the long run. Being crippled by shyness and afraid to face people was now a thing of the past. I had earned my stripes and felt better for it. Much of my repertoire had worked, but there had been a few disasters. That mattered not, the secret had been in the thorough preparation and the practise and for a while I was a popular lad on the block and that was both warming and gratifying.

Much of my spare time was now taken up by entertaining at children's parties. I was also becoming more ambitious in my hobby and purchasing tricks from a London catalogue which were fearfully expensive. My other problem was transport. My father was not always available to take me to venues and getting a loaded case plus hatbox and a new magician's table onto a bus was problematic to say the least. The love of magic would always stay with me, but my interest in it was being diluted by a new hobby, amateur dramatics. The theatre had always been an abiding love but I became smitten by the dream of walking across a stage and speaking lines that someone else had written. I wanted to play a character in a drama, to memorise lines and feel the adrenalin of opening night, to be with fellow actors, in costume, in make-up, to feel the stage lights on my face and the rustle of an audience in the auditorium, gripped by the action and ready to applaud. How I loved the applause and the adoration from the crowds. It felt good and it felt so right.

***

My world of magic became my world of live theatre, for I was now an active member of two town dramatic societies. In one we performed *The Witch* – a Norwegian play, translated into English by John Masefield and set in 16th-century Bergen. My second appearance was in *The Happiest Days of Your Life* by John Dighton, made famous by the 1950s film of the same name starring Alastair Sim and Margaret Rutherford. It became the pre-cursor for all the St Trinian films. I loved it all. Both parts were substantial and the *Happiest Days* was very funny and enjoyed enormously by cast and audience.

What had happened to the shy, introverted lad who had trembled in his boots at the thought of facing anyone and was now seeking the limelight wherever he could find it? I was totally gripped; nothing else was more important in my life than playing to an audience. The daily drudgery of work in an office became unbearable as I pondered the possibility of life in the professional theatre; the applause, the curtain calls, the smell of greasepaint, signing autograph books. It was a world I longed to be part of, to be in a professional theatre and to join the ranks of actors eager to entertain a live audience. Not that I would refuse parts on television, you understand. I would learn to become adaptable, find myself an agent who would find me work. As far as I could see, the future was bright and the West End lay in wait for my imminent arrival.

***

Sidcup is a small town in the London Borough of Bexley in south-east England and now part of Greater London. It is sometimes referred to as 'the gateway to Kent' and was known primarily for being part of Edward Heath's constituency of Sidcup and Old Bexley. He was Prime Minister from 1970 to 1974. Today, Sidcup has high-rise offices and apartments. In 1960, the suburbia of the 1930s still shone through: smart semi-detached housing with green trees. Most people living there commuted to London, Bromley, Streatham and Lewisham on a daily basis. In fact, Sidcup's railway station is reputed to be the place where Mick Jagger and Keith Richards decided to form the band which went on to become The Rolling Stones. In 1959, something or someone prompted me to consider training to be an actor in a college suited for the purpose. I read somewhere about such a place in Sidcup, sent for the prospectus, applied and was called to attend an audition. The desire to become a professional actor was almost painful yet the thought of attending an audition in front of English strangers miles from Aberystwyth in deepest Kent was beginning to trouble me. In fact I was sick with worry, but calmed myself with the thought that if Richard Burton had achieved status and brought fame to Port Talbot and Pontrhydyfen, there was no reason why I should not do the same for Aberystwyth and my village.

One factor continues to puzzle me: my father actually allowed me to attend this audition. He, who had been so protective of me throughout my childhood, proclaimed that it was my life and that I should choose how to live it. The Cardiganshire Education Department were promising a grant and my father stood by ready to support me where necessary. I am sure the family went without to accommodate this passion of mine but, in my wildest dreams, I did not seriously expect to get through the audition. Our father was heard to say to a friend, "If David wants to leave home, why doesn't he try to find a proper job?" My father never uttered those words to me but remained loyal to the belief that I would, one day, make him feel proud. As I contemplated the audition, my skin became worse and unbelievably, the old nerves returned in traditional style.

***

If I succeeded in passing the audition, the preparation for such a course was immense. My father looked at the list of requirements and bit his lip. There was a complete kit and a library of books that he would have to pay for: Homer's *Odyssey, English Verse – Volumes 1 to 5, The Complete Shakespeare, Voice and Speech in the Theatre.* There were books required on early Greek theatre, the history of British theatre, medieval and restoration drama. There were textbooks on the actor's preparation and the techniques involved. I would be required to learn about costume, stage design, choral speaking, mime, acting in comedy and tragedy and Greek dancing. Poetry and public speaking came in abundance, as did books on the production of voice, stage fighting, microphone and camera techniques and the works of Jung, Freud, Stanislavski, and the material for wigs and moustaches with bottles of spirit gum and tins of cream to remove the wretched stuff. There were books on movement, mime and stage delivery and study of the lungs and the larynx, the tongue, the teeth and lips – all the bits required for speaking which I had never thought of in the past. My father would be compelled to pay for an expensive trunk that would be sent to my digs, ahead of the journey, should I prove to be a successful candidate and, if successful, I would need black tights, black ballet shoes, black short-sleeve shirts, black bathing costume, a black cloak and a jock strap. The final item produced more laughter in the family than any other. My young sister was quick to mock the afflicted.

"Will you be wearing your jockie strap every day, David?" she said, with a grin which set us all howling with laughter.

The day of the audition arrived and on reaching Sidcup I was immediately sick in someone's front garden. My mouth remained dry all day and my colour a ghastly ashen. The nerves, which had long been banished, returned with a vengeance. The pastoral location of the college fronting a mirror-glass lake did nothing for my confidence.

There were around a hundred other young people in attendance at the audition, some with cut-glass accents, courtesy of family background and public schooling, others were straight up from the sticks like myself. From as far afield as Tyneside, Scotland, Dorset, Devon, Cornwall, London, the Midlands and Wales; we all fancied our chances as actors and for those who did not, there was opportunity to do a teacher's diploma in speech and drama. We were told by the second-year students who were showing us around, that regional accents were not acceptable and that, if successful in becoming one of the chosen few, every effort would be made to help us speak with a standard English voice. Whatever that meant, I was none too sure. I had never bothered to listen to the way I spoke. I just spoke and that was it.

I had been asked to prepare three audition pieces for the tutors. I chose one of Danny's speeches from *Night Must Fall*, a spooky tale of a psychopath, by Emlyn Williams. Another from Shakespeare's *Henry V*, which I had studied for my school certificate. My choice of poetry was 'The Song of the Shirt' by Thomas Hood (1799–1845), a poem I had learned in school, but a shortage of material compelled me to revisit it for this college test. The pieces were about murder, conquest, death and grinding poverty. Sadly, I felt I delivered them badly; moreover I smelt of vomit which must have been off-putting for the adjudicators and candidates alike. The tutors, both men and women, were well groomed, young and precise, with voices that sounded English and important. They looked upon me with interest, smiled politely and tolerated my mistakes with a wave of the hand. This was not home and I felt I was being scrutinized, questioned and talked about behind closed doors. When asked what acting I had done, I mentioned the amateur companies at home. They nodded and smiled condescendingly. I remember thinking that they must have heard of them, or had they not?

We were asked to act out improvisations with some of the other candidates and it then became obvious they could act just as well as me, if not a darned sight better. Their performances were more polished and more convincing and they looked altogether more 1960s than I did. I was a country lad with a thick Cardiganshire accent but not much shine when it came to the sophistication and nous of some of the other candidates. I returned to join my mother in the High Street later that day, feeling positively shredded and drained. I would not, I believed, be seeing that place again and welcomed the return journey home to Aberystwyth.

***

Weeks passed and the letter from the Rose Bruford College of Speech and Drama finally arrived. I could not believe my eyes. I had passed my audition. How I qualified for entry to this establishment puzzles me to this day. Maybe those posh tutors had seen something I was oblivious to: whatever the reason, it was now all hands on deck to get me ready to leave home and move down to digs in Sidcup. Did I really want to go? In some ways yes, and in others, no. I looked at my home and all that I held close to my heart: my family, the woods, the trees, the beaches, the fields. There were all my friends in Aberystwyth and my colleagues. The place where I was born. It was time to say goodbye to all of it, and I couldn't for the life of me find the words.

A friend of mine from Cardiff, Dr John Maynard, who went through a similar experience and became a drama student and actor before returning to education and gaining his Ph.D., has his own overview about our struggles and ambitions in those late 1950s and early 1960s:

> We were brought up in those post-war years and became accustomed to the tedium of the early 1950s. There was not much money and our lives were lived against a background of shortages and economic post-war depression. We did as our fathers and mothers had done before us, and the future seemed blighted with a nine to five existence and not much else. The cultural revolution which started in the middle to late 1950s changed all that, as we questioned what had gone before. Some of us wanted something new, something different. A new set of challenges lay before us and the arts were exciting and glamorous and worth striving for.

In my view, John is right. The future did look brighter. Attitudes were changing and these changes were reflected in the way we lived, in music, the arts and literature. The changes were certainly obvious on the English stage, where a new breed of dramatists was making a difference: John Osborne, Harold Pinter, Arnold Wesker, Shelagh Delaney. All had something new to say and had a challenging new way of saying it. We were experiencing a realism in acting and literature that had not been seen or read before; the anti-heroes were shredding our old values and asking new questions. Keith Waterhouse with his *Billy Liar* and Alan Sillitoe with *The Loneliness of the Long-Distance Runner* and *Saturday Night and Sunday Morning*. There was John Osborne's *Luther* and *Look Back in Anger* plus

The L-Shaped Room by Lynne Reid Banks. The austere post-war years and the early 1960s were revealing changes in our social culture. Popular music had radically changed and the cinema was equally reflective, with actors from the American schools of method acting like Marlon Brando. *A Streetcar Named Desire* (US, 1951) and *On the Waterfront* (US, 1954), touch all my senses at the same time. They did then and they still do now. *On the Waterfront* went on to win eight Oscars and a further three Oscar nominations. In the words of Professor Yahnke, professor of Film and Arts at the University of Minnesota:

> These films were about believable characters whose conflicts are more inward than outward. Acting in film would never be the same again. Brando sighed, brooded, grimaced, moaned and mumbled. He was the character.

Brando was followed by so many more.

My father was a wise old bird. I would like to think that he was fully aware of the changes that were taking place and he had hoped that, within it all, there would be a place for me. He gave me every encouragement, sent me money when times were tough and always emphasised that there was a place for me back home if ever I wanted to give up the chase.

So, I had made my decision. I was 20 and I was leaving home for the first time. Was it the right decision, I wondered. Only the future would tell and, after my years in training, that was as uncertain as the profession I was planning to enter.

CHAPTER 3

"Breathe my Darlings, and Swing those Ribs"

IT WAS AUTUMN and as John Keats mused, the 'season of mists and mellow fruitfulness'. My grandmother shed a tear as I slipped down the road out of sight on that September morning in 1960, leaving my family on the doorstep waving and believing that life would never be quite the same again in our little house at the top of the hill.

I was leaving home for the first time in my life to become a student at the Rose Bruford Training College of Speech and Drama. The unquenchable desire to become a professional actor was telling me this was the right path to take; there was not a grain of doubt in my mind. To be chosen out of hundreds, possibly thousands of other applicants to the college, was indeed a rare privilege.

***

I felt Sidcup in Kent was the other side of the world. My digs were spacious. A large 1930s house in suburban Sidcup at the end of an apparently endless street. The heating was minimal, with large squat paraffin heaters in the living room where we sat at the table and received our breakfast and evening meal from a hatch in the wall. Five other lads, four of whom sounded very English, were at the table that night and I was the last to arrive, my Welsh accent causing some amusement.

I shared a cold bedroom with Gerald from Ripon who spoke with a Yorkshire accent so thick, I could barely understand him. He was a nice lad but, alas, knew little about personal hygiene. The smell coming from our bedroom must have kept the mice at bay. I dreaded him going to bed. When those socks came off, the stench was intolerable. I lay there in my bed with my head under the pillow trying to avoid the unpleasant odour of his stale perspiration. Mind you, we bathed only once a week. To bathe twice a week would have been unrealistic. The gas meter consumed too many shilling pieces, and life on a college grant was precipitously tight.

There were four other students, all friendly enough lads. Michael had a square attractive face and reminded me of Welsh actor, Glyn Houston. He was always looking for an argument with the others. Peter was tall, debonair and lantern jawed, with dark hair that fell across his forehead. Bernard, from Hastings, had smooth English tones to his voice; his face was distinctive – in my humble opinion he was destined for bigger things. Francis had a consumptive appearance with a flat, Roman-style haircut. He was slimmer than the rest of us and quite 'camp' and I loved the way he could dismiss irrelevant argument with a comical toss of his head.

Mrs Blaney, our landlady, complete with headscarf, ran the house with meticulous efficiency only appearing at meal times through a hatch in the wall when it was time to serve the food and collect our rent of three pounds, ten shillings a week. Did she live in there I wondered and how short or tall was she? I only saw her through the hatch. We ate and worked collectively in that spacious living room. The bedrooms were either too cold or too smelly, for after two weeks in our first term the stench from the socks was beginning to penetrate the very fabric of the building and bedroom doors were kept firmly shut. The college prospectus proudly proclaimed its future with words written for it by college friend and Poet Laureate, John Masefield:

... Beauty awaits man's capture, as of old:
She waits you here; adventure and be bold.
... May all your pupils have success
Increasing England's loveliness,
Making her future bright.

Well, who could argue with that? My future was assured. The great man himself had said so. Look out England, here I come. Such names as Sir Laurence Olivier and Dame Peggy Ashcroft were friends of the college and that in itself endorsed the greatness of the establishment.

The first day was organised chaos with kit inspection. All the boys displayed their kit including their black jockstraps with nametags, and the girls, their kit including black knickers were held high in the air as tutors checked each item. Black cloaks were checked, black aertex shirts, black shorts, black tights, black ballet shoes, black make-up tin. Black was the fashionable shade and if someone had called a funeral, we would have been strangely but suitably attired. Everything was checked and double-checked by staff and second-year students. Spirit gum for false beard and moustaches, make-up remover, make-up sticks, eyebrow pencils and enough books and files to fill the National Library and all of it tagged and numbered; I remembered thinking of all the prisoner-of-war films I had seen – it seemed there were similarities! This establishment was going to flatten our characters and personalities and rebuild them with the leftovers. What a bunch of misfits we must have looked, straight out of the ark with strangulated dialects and enough attitudes to sink the *Queen Mary*.

When lectures began, my brain was assailed from every quarter with subjects that were totally foreign to me. What went on in ancient Thebes became mixed in with Oliver Goldsmith and William Congreve. Chekhov and Stanislavski paired off quite nicely but Oscar Wilde and Euripides made little sense. In one lecture I was up to my elbows in 'size' – a gluey substance for applying to stage scenery prior to painting it – in another, trying to widen my lower ribs to disproportionate levels and pant on my diaphragm. Where the hell was my diaphragm? I couldn't find it. My tongue refused to lie flat for the 'ah' sound and my 'ee' sound was produced through lips so tight that they stretched from one ear to the other. A bad habit that required immediate attention! Were they going to put me under the knife I wondered? To make matters worse, it was pointed out that my 'a' sound was hard and detestable: it was not 'cat' or 'mat' with a hard 'a' sound but 'caet' or 'maet' with the blade of the tongue in a more raised position. If I had sported dentures, the inside of my mouth would have been a real mess. I did more tongue humping exercise than I care to remember and as for glottal stops and the sibilant 's' – it appeared we all had those and they were instantly condemned to the knackers' yard. The problem was if we didn't have a 'sibilant s' to start with, we sure had one by the end of the week.

Sister Suzie sewing socks for soldiers.
She sells sea shells on the sea shore.
Which switch, Miss, is the right switch for Ipswich Miss?
Which witch wished which wicked wish?

We were told that we were being taught to speak in 'standard English'. There was no room for dialect or localised accents. If we were to be professional actors, we should be adaptable in our speech and speak in any accent that the play required, and from a level playing field that meant no accent at all. What was 'standard English' please? Could someone please explain? Was it the way royalty spoke? Was it the way they sounded on the BBC? Was it what I regarded as 'posh'? I did not believe I had any accent but I was told by all those from England that it was obvious the moment I opened my mouth: pure Cardiganshire lilt and it had to go.

"Amidst the mists and coldest frost, with stoutest wrists and loudest boasts, he thrusts his fists against the posts and still insists he sees the ghosts."

Shakespeare, Browning, Betjeman and Bunyan became intermingled with Masefield, Matthew Arnold and Walter de la Mare; as for Pinero and Strindberg, I was now genuinely confused. The pace of learning was unremitting and my homework on the increase. There was just enough time to go and see *Dr No* in the High Street, with this government agent called James Bond killing a deadly spider in his bedroom. Breathing and humming on the lips, to increase forward resonance, became second nature. We hummed everywhere. We hummed as we walked home at the end of an exhausting day and we hummed as we went to bed. I missed my home in Aberystwyth where there was comfort and warmth... and no humming required.

Many mighty men making much money in the moonshine.

There were seven or eight lectures a day with the greatest concentration on voice, speech and movement. There were generous amounts of verse speaking, all of which had to be learned off by heart. Also English literature, history of poetry, theatre, drama and costume, social history, education and psychology, music, singing, Greek dancing, mime, making and adapting stage costume and accessories, make-up. There was public speaking, improvisation, stage craft, radio and television technique and phonetics. Inflexible bodies were bent in every direction; mime and Greek dancing became second nature and then there was fencing with a German gentleman who stretched our arms and legs further than we had ever stretched before. Maybe he had been the commandant in my imaginary prisoner-of-war camp. We developed supple sinews and aching joints. We were constantly undressing and changing our apparel for whatever lecture was coming up next. We sat in these lectures with our black cloaks tightly wrapped around us to keep warm after sweating profusely in the previous movement lecture. Young limbs ached with exercise and voices could be heard practising:

MAH NAH LAH, MAY NAY LAY, MEEN NEE LEE, MAY NAY LAY, MA NA LA, MAW NAW LAW, MOO NOO LOO, MAW NAW LAW.

Try saying that at speed after a few glasses of wine. We whispered, then voiced: "Father's car is a jaguar and pa drives rather fast. Castles, farms and draughty barns, we go charging past."

The problem most of us had was with our breathing – not sufficient breath to carry the spoken word. So we embarked on a thing called 'intercostal diaphragmatic breathing'. WHAT? And yet, we smoked. It was the done thing. We were allowed to smoke in lectures. Even the lecturers themselves smoked. The whole country smoked and lighting up after some thumping limb stretching exercise was common practice. It was deep breathing one minute and a packet of ten Gold Leaf the next.

Who are you sir, tell me who? What's that to you sir? Who Sir? You Sir. What's that to you Sir? Who Sir? You!

Our voices were being trained to carry to the back of the theatre auditorium without strain and without pain. We had to learn to walk on stage, enter and exit through doors, sit, cry, listen, stage fight and wrestle, and be everything from trees in meadows to children in playpens. As for improvisation, acting a plot without script, a basic actor's requirement, try this one when you have nothing else to do:

Mum is sitting in the living room playing with their first infant by the open fire. Dad is at the table counting his monthly takings. Mum goes upstairs to discover that the second infant has drowned in the bath. She screams out in horror and Dad goes rushing up to see what the problem is. They both come downstairs heartbroken, only to discover that the first infant has thrown all the paper money on the fire and the living room is ablaze.

Well, that one sorted us out. I had never seen so many variations of a family going insane.

***

"If the two-two to Tooting was too soon to hoot, would the two get to Tooting as soon as the hoot?"

My clothes took on a new look. I noticed the other boys wearing trousers that were tighter fitting. Out went the floppy turn-ups, so common on men in the 1950s, and in came the sleek, 1960s tapered look. I even sported a dickey bow like other students on the course, and on occasions I wore a cravat. How daring was that?

Maid Marion made a maddening mess of the mash.

My father had warned me against men who had leanings towards other men. Now I must admit that was a new one on me. Somehow this became less of an issue in drama college, not that I was 'queer', as it was called in those days, but tolerance towards gay people in the acting profession was something we all took on board as a matter of course. Rumours abounded. Rumours about the staff and rumours about other students in the upper years and rumours about famous actors. It was all salaciously undercover but discussed from time to time by the students in our digs and in the college common room. Some of us adopted a rather 'camp' air – not to signify that we were gay, although the word 'gay' in those days, had a different meaning, but to imply that we were, "Moving in theatrical circles, darling, and understanding life with all its many platitudes." If putting my weight on one leg with a bent knee and having a limp wrist was slightly affected, it was because I was playing a rather foppish gentleman in a segment of a 17th-century play.

Only God would know what they would be saying back home in Aberystwyth!

When I arrived home on that Aberystwyth station platform at the end of my first term, my mother and sister were horrified to see me in tapered trousers and dickey bow. I was carrying a tightly rolled-up umbrella and shouted across at them in a most extravagantly accentuated Chelsea voice, "Hello mother darling, hello Jean, how are you both?" I openly mouthed the words. The voice tutors had pressed it home time and time again the importance of clean, forward vowel sounds based on an open jaw that produced a sound perfect in tone and resonance. The following day, my mother, showing less patience towards my somewhat contrived way of speaking, threw up her arms in exasperation and shouted, "For God's sake David, talk properly for a change." I was mortified and could not understand why my new voice was not being appreciated by everyone at home. My father declared I was as, "soft as pudding", and hid himself behind a newspaper. To escape further criticism, I took to the hills behind my home and projected my speeches and voice exercises to the sheep: Bernard Shaw, Oscar Wilde, Shakespeare, the lake poets, Winston Churchill's war speeches, Henry V at Agincourt, Elizabeth I at Tilbury Fort. Never before had the local sheep received such high entertainment. I felt like charging them admission.

***

At the end of each term, there were plays to perform to our fellow students and at the end of each year, an end-of-year production on a grand scale. This consisted of a play that could accommodate a multitude of students on a West End stage such as Sadler's Wells. The plum parts went to the top students in the third year who were hoping that London agents would be present in the auditorium to watch their performances. The rest of us were in the crowd scenes, over-acting like mad, and in the stage management teams that humped heavy rostra and scenery from one side of the stage to the other. The task was enormous, the stage vast and the auditorium like a huge open mouth waiting to devour young drama students. There were hundreds of costumes and props, a million lighting and sound cues, and stuff being flown in from the grid, the gantry above the stage from where lamps were suspended. There was also a steel thunder sheet hanging from the grid, which when shaken produced some awesome thunder claps. Golgotha was not Golgotha without thunder claps. Whoever had that job was on to a winner – no prancing about in frocks and sandals lifting staggeringly heavy rostra.

I had one line in *The Dark Hours* – a play about the crucifixion. It went, "When we come early, we have time to eat." I worried about this line. My mother informed me once that she had been in a play in which she had to utter the words, "Is it?" When the crucial time came, her mouth opened and out came, "It is." The rest of the cast looked on helplessly. I suffered with the unimaginable nightmare in which I would walk onto the Sadler's Wells stage and, instead of saying," When we come early we have time to eat," out would come, "When we are late, we eat too early." What a disaster that would be. I would wake up in a sweat at night. It was a throw-away line but I felt there were a hundred different way of saying it. Also, should I sound like Shylock from the *Merchant of Venice* or like an Israelite who could eat a horse? I was told by our principal/producer to make the character less Welsh sounding. So much for my voice exercises in front of the sheep.

Every night we applied body make-up to our arms and legs. If Christ was going to be crucified by the Jews, we had to look biblically Jewish: pale skins had to look bronzed and the hot and arid country brought on warts and all. Trying to move the Garden of Eden in desert costume, with the lights out, dressed in biblical sandals, was like moving around the stage in molasses. We received a lecture from the principal about body odour. "There is no excuse for it in our college. The chemist down the road has a plentiful supply of nice smells."

Let us hope that Gerald, the student from our digs, is taking heed! For months after, the college smelt like a branch of Boots the Chemist.

> ... and the best test of the breath test is that the best breath stands the breath tests best.

We were told there were no small parts, only small actors. If you were on the stage in a scene with no lines to speak, you listened and reacted to what was being said by the lead actors. I could remember reading somewhere about an early Richard Burton performance on a London or Stratford stage in which he stood there, saying nothing, and the audience were riveted and spellbound watching him. This could be my lucky break!

The technical runs where you have to repeatedly stop and start acting in order that lighting could be planned and plotted drove us wild with all the hanging around. We would be on that stage from 8 a.m. to 11 p.m. For actors under training, this was the hardest part of being an actor and if anyone showed signs of weakness, we were immediately reprimanded. This was no picnic, it was hard slog. It was believing in an art form and sticking to it despite the drawbacks and pitfalls, the pain and the agony. We had to learn to suffer for our art and being an actor and experiencing the hardship was all part of living an actor's life.

***

One guest lecturer was Shakespearean actor, Richard Ainley, son of the great Edwardian actor, Henry Ainley. Richard was severely disabled in the war and had a withered arm and a slight stoop but his vocal quality was a treat to behold. The richest of voices that on a mere whisper could be heard at the back of the Barn theatre. This man went on to teach Albert Finney, Tom Courtenay and Diana Rigg.

My fellow students were all roughly in my age group, in

their 20s or just under, and the majority from middle-class backgrounds. There were the exceptions, of course: those with private education behind them, complete with cut-glass English accents and a nifty style in clothing. They always looked down their noses at me and were infuriatingly stylish and brusque. I was someone from the coal mines. I had the devil's own job trying to explain to other students that there were no coal mines in Aberystwyth. Relics of lead ones outside the town, but no coal.

The college's curriculum was like facing the north ridge of Everest without the climbing equipment. Reaching diploma level in acting and teaching in this college was not going to be a bed of roses. The amount of work that lay ahead was grimly daunting but the theatre was my chosen career and it would take nothing short of wild horses to drag me away from that thought. I was not the only one with such goals. There were 56 students in my year, with another 120 or so spread across other years and, apart from those few who wanted to teach, we all had one driving ambition. To become professional actors.

***

The end of term would arrive but all thoughts of having a restful break would be banished by last minute instructions. Weaknesses would be highlighted and we were told in no uncertain terms what work was required and what improvements were expected by the beginning of the new term.

"Breathe my darlings, and swing those ribs David Lloyd, and practise those vowel sounds again and again. Work to maintain a relaxed poise, controlled breathing, and open jaw, a well-placed forward tongue. Hum till your lips buzz and no Welsh accent next term, PLEASE!"

I guess it was back to the sheep!

CHAPTER 4

The Humming Birds

ROSE BRUFORD, HON. R.A.M. had a list of academic achievements to her name as long as my arm: performer, teacher, producer, author, membership of various institutes and examining bodies, qualifications in performance, voice, speech, mime, Greek dancing, fencing with foils and phonetics. I remember her words so clearly:

"The stage is a tough place to be and actors and actresses (as it was put in those days) must expect a tough life. Do not expect the theatre to be handed to you on a plate. In this, your second year, we will be expecting high standards from you all. Tomorrow you will be 'holding the mirror up to nature' as it were, reflecting all that you have learned. Good acting does not just happen. It comes through hard work and sacrifice. We give you much and we will expect much from you in return."

As Miss Bruford promised, my second year in college was tough and relentless. To make matters worse, I could do little to win the praise of my class tutors. I was not the only one. Francis, back in our digs, complained bitterly and made his announcement one evening.

"Darlings, I just can't do this. I mean, look at me. I'm in a f*****g mess and can't sleep at nights. All these bloody books and all those lecture notes, I am running myself ragged – even my hair is falling out."

He dragged contemptuously on his cigarette and minced out of the room. We just sat there roaring with laughter but not admitting to the fact we were all going through our own private hell. Of calamitous moments, I had many, but one remains vivid in my memory. This particular moment would make me the laughing stock of the college. To demonstrate our teaching ability, we were asked to prepare a mime lesson for a class of children. The children on this occasion would be my fellow students. Also present in the class was a pianist and Rose Bruford herself with an assistant tutor. They sat at the back, solid, solemn and dignified. I applied my new-found skill of forward-planning and prepared, on paper, a detailed analysis of the lesson's introduction, its development and its happy conclusion. Everyone had to imagine themselves as underwater creatures or objects in a large sea. Arms and legs were brought into play as my friends mimed the movement of different species of fish. Some were even rocks on the seabed, taking up the position of... well... rocks on the seabed! Everything was going swimmingly and the piano music was cascadingly effective as each student listened to my commentary and mimed life under the water – animal, vegetable and mineral. And then came the unimaginable moment which, even today, has me occasionally waking up, thrashing and coming out in a cold sweat:

"You are now an octopus and we all know what an octopus is like. A large oval, flabby body with eight long TESTICLES. Feel your TESTICLES flowing freely in the currents of water around you. Suddenly you spot your next tasty morsel, and stretch your TESTICLES out towards it..."

There was a rather loud but muffled snigger from the back of the class, which developed into open hysteria amongst the students. Miss Bruford was beginning to look thunderstruck and annoyingly agitated. My immediate thought was that my classroom 'pupils' were misbehaving in order to test my abilities in classroom control.

"OK," I said. "Enough is enough. We have all enjoyed a good laugh. Let us now return to the matter in hand and think about our TESTICLES."

The laughter became an uproar. The fact that I was confusing my TESTICLES with my TENTACLES did not occur to my bird brain. The greater my attempt to rescue the lesson, the more the situation became uncontrollable – students rolling around on the floor in hysterical agony and the tutors lost and unsure what to say or do. As I kept on yelling 'TESTICLES', I could see Miss Bruford, a confirmed spinster of the parish of Foots Cray, rise like a phoenix and command the class to an immediate return to order. She had to choose her next seven words with care.

"SILENCE! David, the word is, tentacles. TENTACLES," she spat out in a well-articulated voice. The bittersweet smile on her face indicated a woman with her first real major challenge in teaching, and I had provided it. Needless to say, I became the most popular student in my year and was frequently greeted with the words, "Hello David boyo. How's your testicles this morning?"

**

My various landladies and the digs they provided would command a book all to themselves, but space does not allow me such luxury. Sharing a room became overbearingly difficult and, like the other boys, I wanted my own independence. Move number two was to a house that, on the surface, seemed pleasant enough. It was situated in a leafy road with rose borders and well-trimmed hedges. With everything compact and neatly laid out, Mrs Joylan seemed the archetypal great aunt. A lined face with a smile to please, she had snow white hair and was of small stature. This time I had a large bedroom with an ample amount of space. The house was petite, like Mrs Joylan herself, with country cottage furniture and fittings. Behind the house, there was a long garden in which I could practise my lines, walking the length of it slowly time after time, helping them to stick in my memory. Mrs Joylan claimed her daughter, Mary, was slightly disturbed, but begged me not to take any notice of anything unusual in her nature. I was intrigued but discovered on meeting her, a pretty lady with a rather remote personality and a slight stammer. Her eyes would gaze upward and she would grow tired of the conversation she was having with me and retire to her bedroom. One night, as I lay in bed, I awoke to a blazing row going on downstairs between mother and daughter. The following morning revealed nothing new and my breakfast was served with the usual courtesies. "We are both well thank you, David. Mary had a lovely night with her friends and I went to a social. We came in late and crept upstairs so as not to disturb you." That, I feared, was a lie and later that week, Mrs Joylan took me aside and apologised for Mary's behaviour, making no reference to the late-night row I had heard earlier that week. My worry was not with Mary but with Mrs Joylan herself. There was something not quite right with her and it troubled me. Some months later, all was revealed in a rather nasty way. It was my 21st birthday, celebrated without much fuss as later that week I was travelling home. It was the end of term and the end-of-term productions were in full swing. I arrived home quite late to pack away all my birthday cards and gifts. I went up and down the stairs on tiptoe, deciding to pack my case in the lounge rather than disturb the sleeping women upstairs. As I walked across the small hallway to the stairs for the fourth time, there, up on the landing, stood a frenzied Mrs Joylan looking down at me, her face etched with rage. She was dressed in a white, full-length nightdress and her hair was in a tangled mess. The mad woman from *Jane Eyre* flashed across my mind.

"What bloody time do you think this is?" Mrs Joylan shouted. I was startled by her language.

"Yes, I'm sorry," I replied. "I'm sorry for any noise; it's 11.30… it's late… I'm off to bed now."

"This is not good enough," she snapped, moving slowly down the stairs towards me. "This is definitely not good enough. You have no respect for my house or my privacy. You are a slovenly moron and I cannot take any more of you."

"Mrs Joylan, please. I am neither slovenly nor, what you

call, a moron." I stepped back, shocked at this outburst, but decided to defend my corner in the best way I could.

"Mrs Joylan… for the short time I have been here, I have had nothing but respect for you, your daughter and your property."

Her voice rose to an even higher pitch.

"Don't talk to me like that and don't talk to me about my daughter. Only I know what is best for her." She was now looking frighteningly menacing. "I hate everything you stand for. You have taken every advantage of me and I feel defenceless against you. You cannot live here any longer. I hate it. Get out at once!"

Mrs Joylan was quite mad, I was convinced of that. I tried to reason with her. I explained that I intended to leave in the morning and I would not be returning. Would she please allow me time to pack all my things now and book a taxi for 8 a.m. She hit me across the chest, tears coming down her face.

"Get out of my house you scumbag. Leave my house and my life. Mary and I can cope extremely well without your sort around." She turned and ran upstairs, slamming the bedroom door behind her.

I made a taxi call at 6 a.m. and booked a car for 7.30. As I eased my way out of the front door I spotted two bedroom doors open simultaneously. I backed my way towards the front gate and the waiting taxi. Mrs Joylan had come down the stairs and was gently closing the front door behind me. I loaded my luggage into the car and sat back in the vehicle with a large measure of relief. As the car pulled away I looked back and, in the upstairs window, Mrs Joylan and her daughter Mary were waving slowly between the nets, their faces pale, like ghosts and without expression.

I have often pondered about Mrs Joylan and her daughter, Mary. Now, 50 years on, I still think of them from time to time. What became of them I wonder? Was there some form of psychiatric imbalance in them both. Were they slightly out of synch with reality? What had happened to them in the past to have caused such strange patterns of behaviour? Despite their hideous rows, they both lived together and I was the intruder they could not accept. I told the college welfare officer about my experience in the house and the strange behaviour patterns. To my knowledge, no other students were sent there.

***

My knowledge of London was now comparable with my knowledge of my home town. In some way the college was responsible. Every effort was made to encourage us to visit London theatres. The seats, alas, were not the best in the house but they were the best we could afford. We sat in the 'Gods' or with the 'Gods'(!), looking down from a vast distance to the tiny stage below – but what a treat that was. I saw the original cast of Lionel Bart's *Oliver* with Ron Moody, Georgia Brown and Paul Whitson-Jones stomping up 2,618 performances with a wooden, revolving turntable set designed by Sean Kenny. If the London stage had not done particularly well since the Second World War, the sun was about to shine on it with three spectacular musicals, namely *Oliver, Stop the World I Want to Get Off* with young Anthony Newley singing 'What Kind of Fool am I?' and *Half a Sixpence* with Tommy Steele. I also went to see Lionel Bart's *Blitz* at the Garrick, where London's East End was devastated by bombs in the Second World War and the whole thing was being repeated on stage.

Highly recommended by Miss Bruford herself, was *Waiting in the Wings* starring college patron, Dame Sybil Thorndike and her husband, Sir Lewis Casson.

> Study the way she moves across the stage and picks up that letter on the table. Watch her read it and before placing it back down on the table, she casually glances at the back of the letter to see if anything is written there – it's a casual piece of business but a believable one.

A few of us plucked up the courage to go around to the stage door to greet Dame Sybil as she came out. She was a gracious lady and very polite. When we told her we were Rose Bruford students, she smiled and said sweetly, "Ah yes, how lovely; tell me, how is dear Rose?"

Out of all my West End theatre visits in those days, Donald Pleasance playing the tramp in Pinter's *Caretaker* was probably the most memorable. There are only three characters in the play, but it was an all-star cast with Alan Bates and Robert Shaw playing the two brothers. No one can make pauses in dialogue like Harold Pinter. Albert Finney in *Luther* enthralled us, especially when he threw himself out of the pulpit. We had been studying stage falls in college.

We always discussed what plays we had been to see. "Darling, I thought she was ghastly," said Francis, on the way home on the train from Charing Cross. "That ridiculous hairdo and the way she tripped over the carpet. It was so false."

"But that's what you would do given that situation," argued Peter. "It's called, 'seeking the truth'."

"Rubbish darling, absolute rubbish."

And so the weeks ran into terms. Time slipped by without our knowing. The work intensified, both practical and theoretical. We learned to teach young children one day and how to study a part in a medieval play the next; how to walk across the stage and sit; to listen to a telephone ring, or a door bell, to open and close a door. To sit, to cry, to grieve, to kiss, to fall; to feel cold and heat, to express anger, love, hatred and expose raw emotion was not easy. How to play a rogue, a harlot, a pimp, a rich man or a poor man. We studied old age and youth: we gazed at people outside on the street until it became embarrassing. All the things we had learned to do from an early age came under the microscope. To repeat all those things again on a stage in front of an audience took training. Most importantly, to find the truth in a part and, in some cases, that took some finding. The voice lessons continued as did the history of theatre and costume and everything else that went with it, including speaking in public. In an end-of-term production I was playing a major role in a Moliere play and at the end of my second year, it would be *Cyrano de Bergerac* at Sadler's Wells again. Then came another knock that sent shock waves through my body; its reverberations would be felt many years hence.

***

Frederick Parker was a retired classical actor who understood every facet of theatre. He had devoted his life to acting and production and was doubtless treading the boards before I was born. His voice, although slightly raspy with age, was still clear and distinct. In college staff circles I believe he considered himself one of yesterday's top dogs and still fully capable of producing and directing a production. His suit was always slightly shorter in length than his height; his trousers were invariably half-mast and his jacket sleeves too short.

He was taking us in the art of theatre directing and we had been instructed to choose a play and direct a segment of it, using our own colleagues as the cast. My turn approached and I glanced down at my immaculately prepared prompt copy of my chosen play which was *Ghost Train* by Arthur Ridley, who happened to be the white-haired old actor from *Dad's Army*.

"Right Welsh boy, let's see what you can do," Frederick requested, looking across the room at me with doubt and suspicion written across his face and a slight hint of scepticism in his voice. My cast rose from their seats and took their position on stage. I gave them an idea of where we were in the play's development and proceeded to plot their moves and help them on the delivery of their lines.

"STOP! STOP! STOP!" shouted Frederick, the anger rising in his command. "What do you think you are doing Welsh boy?"

I was annoyed on two counts. One, that he had stopped me so soon in the rehearsal and two, calling me 'Welsh boy' was designed to make his audience of students snigger. He loved posing for the girls and winking at the boys. He had his favourites, did Frederick, and I was not one of them. I was bringing my actors forward into their own spotlights in order to create a ghostly atmosphere on this lonely country station platform.

"How stupid, can you be? Can you not see the one cardinal sin you have committed?"

"No, sir," I responded.

"All your actors are in a straight line on the stage. Can you not be more imaginative with your plotting you brainless boy."

"But they are there for a reason," I explained. "They are standing on a platform waiting for a train and..."

Frederick was now in a 'theatrical' temper and he was making sure everyone knew it.

"Do not argue with me boy. Listen to what I am saying, or are they so brainless in your valley boyo?"

More sniggers.

I argued back and my raised voice got the better of me, which in voice lectures would have secured a certain amount of admiration, but not in Frederick's directing class.

"Please do not call me brainless, Mr Parker. I..."

"Get out of my class, boy. I have no time for you. You have not a clue about theatre and as for directing, forget it. You will never direct anything in your lifetime. GET OUT OF MY CLASS!"

As I made my exit, he turned to the others.

"Bloody thick Welsh."

It produced a feeble laugh. I sat in the college library and contemplated my next move. There was none and as for his racial hatred of the Welsh, well, we could play a winning game of rugby, but the British comedy films of the 1950s had propagated the idea that all Welsh people came from the Valleys and were considered daft. I sat and thought about it for a long time but felt verbally abused.

***

This was my third and final year in the college and, quite frankly, I was worried. Where was I going to find work? I did not want to teach, I wanted to act and my determination to achieve this was as strong as it had been two and half years ago when I left home. I noted that the college prospectus announced '... that the theatrical profession is so overcrowded that the chance of finding consistent employment is slight'. Why had I not paid heed to that clause before leaving home? I discussed it with my family at home and they shared in my concern.

We all read *The Stage* – a weekly newspaper for people working in theatre and television. The college common room always had back copies of *The Stage* and received the weekly editions. I scoured the myriad of advertisements, looking for that all-important job. I wrote to dozens of repertory companies up and down the country asking for an audition in six months' time. They either responded with a generic response which was '... call us nearer the time. We will put your name on our mailing list' or '... sorry, we are already full' or there was often no response at all.

However, another small detail had caught my attention in *The Stage* newspaper. There seemed to be a flurry of excitement in Cardiff all of a sudden. The city in which I had spent the first five years of my life had not changed very much. The trolley buses were still there and the streets were much the same as I remembered them, but there was a certain vibrancy that was echoed in *The Stage*. There was the New Theatre that had a long history, a professional children's company and a caricature theatre who were advertising in *The Stage*. Stan Stennett and Wyn Calvin were frequently in pantomimes and summer shows at Porthcawl. The BBC in Wales were contributing a live play every month to the English network and Television Wales and the West (TWW) and Wales West and North (WWN) – two ITV stations – were up and running and doubtless seeking Welsh talent. There was also a Welsh Theatre Company which played in Cardiff and toured the principality every year. Another important feature, not overlooked by me, was that it was all back home amongst my own people, and that would surely mean something when applying for work.

Rose Bruford told me once that she took her holidays in Gwbert, near Cardigan. I cannot honestly say this piece of news increased our affinity towards each other. I looked up to her. She was the consummate theatre professional, someone who believed in making every sacrifice for their art. If there was pain, she would never feel it and her skill at poetry recital and adjudication was second to none. I saw her, several times, deliver some outstanding work in a beautifully modulated voice and she could hold a hall silent by her presence alone. But there was little love between us and it is likely Rose herself would have said she was not in the business to administer love but to turn out artistes of perfection.

I was two and a half years into my course at Brufords with a negligible response to the numerous letters I was writing to theatres up and down the country seeking work. I felt that moving to Cardiff to complete my training would enhance my opportunities to work in Wales, and yet keep me in touch with London agents and provincial theatres elsewhere. After our initial discussions and putting forward all the solid evidence for moving, Rose called me back some weeks later and informed me that she had secured a place for me to complete my course, subject to interview, at Cardiff's Welsh College of Music and Drama. I was overwhelmed, grateful to her and very excited. In six months, this would put me in the direct line of work in Wales and my chances, I reckoned, would be enhanced. Peter Palmer, my voice tutor at Brufords had also moved to the same college as a senior lecturer and this news also delighted me. I had always got on so well with Peter. I went downstairs to the common room. There was a big cheer; my fellow students had voted me in as deputy head student for 1963 but I did not have the heart to tell them that I would be leaving.

***

As I walked away from the college for the last time on that cold, wintry afternoon, the closing lectures before the Christmas break were in full swing. I looked back and the lights from the large casement windows were reflecting on the cold, tranquil lake. The late afternoon sky had that leaden look and I shivered. I could hear the piano music accompanying the students as they mimed their steps and gestures. And from another room... the constant sound of humming and the chanting of the vowel sounds: all the sounds mixed in together.

From Brufords, I had learned much that was to see me comfortably through my professional life and beyond it. Educationally, I felt stronger and better equipped with an in-depth knowledge of English literature and education, dance and voice. My love of poetry, prose and performance all came from Rose Bruford. I was almost a professional actor with all the new skills that were necessary to survive in the British theatre and that was an achievement to be proud of. Would I get the work, though? That remained my greatest question.

I threw one end of my college scarf over my shoulder, picked up my suitcase and headed for my digs before it started to rain.

***

"Teaching at this college is based on the theory that freedom of movement leads to freedom of speech and that mime and improvisation provide the incentive for good speech without artificiality."

Rose Bruford (1904–1983)

CHAPTER 5

Tin Trays down the Garth

CARDIFF CASTLE, LIKE the town that surrounds it, dates back 2,000 years. In 1948, Harold Hind, director of music at Cardiff City Council, proposed that the Castle be used as a teaching facility for the performing arts. Fifty-three full-time students enrolled. By 1960, the number had doubled. In January 1963, I became the latest addition to the third-year drama intake.

Dr Raymond Edwards, the principal of the college was a man of letters, short and precise, with an educated and cultured, clipped Welsh accent. He was no Rose Bruford, but his encouragement and teaching to a young, working-class lad from Port Talbot produced another of Wales's greatest exports in the world of theatre and cinema, namely Sir Anthony Hopkins. The two men stayed in touch long after Sir Anthony had achieved international fame and, within the new Royal College grounds today, one can see the Anthony Hopkins building, built with monies donated by the great actor. The Royal College, also known as the National Conservatoire of Wales, has grown in stature over the past 60 years, with music and drama students achieving international status. Amongst all the new galleries and studios there now stands the glorious Richard Burton Theatre and the college is justifiably proud. It has become an exciting venue for the performing arts but in 1963 we shared our learning with the city's tourists.

In the castle, lecture rooms were tucked away behind the third Marquis of Bute's and William Burges's medieval Gothic trappings. We crossed highly polished floors and negotiated our way between the baronial banqueting hall, with its fixtures and fittings and crowds of Japanese tourists. Peacocks would wail at us as we clambered up stone steps, around parapets, and through wooden doors to the Black Tower, scene of many historical hauntings but now vibrating to the sound of diaphragmatic intercostal breathing and humming. Peter Palmer, my voice tutor from Brufords, looked up when I entered his lecture room.

"David Lloyd, I taught this man to breathe," he announced to the class with a big welcoming grin on his face. Peter was a wonderful voice teacher and the welcoming students were quite mad in a 'drama student' sort of way and Geraint Morris from Gwaelod y Garth, a small village outside Cardiff, was typical of so many there. Kind, generous and giving with a wonderful sense of humour, Geraint was to play a major part in my life some time later, but I was not to know it then.

The pressure of Brufords had gone and lectures in Cardiff were far more relaxed affairs, and fun and laughter was the order of the day. We performed in London's open-air parks: *Charley's Aunt*, *The Boyfriend* and *The Tinker*. We studied stage fights and had all the girls in class hiding their eyes from the violence and running for the first-aid box. It was the happiest of times and we all relaxed convinced that life outside would be waiting for us with plenty of work for talented, charismatic, up-and-coming actors: I was soon to learn otherwise.

***

Wales West and North (WWN) was a Welsh television channel that operated, with difficulty, to west and parts of north Wales. They wanted some rock and rollers to dance to a pop group they had on their evening magazine programme; could some college students be made available to them? I was chosen amongst others in my year and we were breathless with anticipation. This was our lucky break, or so we thought.

I had been in a television studio before. In my teens, my

Uncle Alex had taken me to see a quiz show being done at Television Wales and the West (TWW). My excitement then was overwhelming. The brightness and the blackness of that studio, the lights, the cameras gliding around effortlessly, the long boom microphone and the unshakeable confidence of Alan Taylor, the presenter. What a famous life he must lead. It was magic. It was the happiest moment of my life; it put me in Hollywood amongst the brightest stars in the firmament and I could not have been a happier teenager. A man waved his arms and told us when to clap and I was totally besotted with the atmosphere. Oh, to be an actor or presenter in front of those huge cameras, I would willingly give everything.

When we walked in as drama students to the WWN studio, my excitement knew no bounds. This was it: this was my moment. I would dance like the best rocker in town and so would all the other students. If I could dance near that camera, there was a good chance my Mum and Dad would see me. Robin Jones sat and read the news at one end of the studio and we waited with the pop group at the other. Our moment came and we danced like never before. My hips swivelled and my body gyrated – I was with it man, so cool and so Sixties. I was sure the whole of Wales had seen me. Three years in drama college, and I had made my first television appearance.

When I rang home my mother was helpless with laughter and quoted my father. "Good God mun! Three years in college and all I could see were his bloody Hush Puppies!"

***

All drama students fell in love. I fell in love. Ridiculously and perilously. Jill came from the music section of the college with a smile to capture my heart and a hand to hold on the darkest of nights. She lived with her parents in Penarth, a place that once housed sea captains and coal owners but had now stretched out its roots to include others who might be slightly better off than the rest of us but not exactly the owners of galleons and coal mines. The house was beautiful with richly carpeted floors and bright, warm living rooms; quite different from my stark, freezing cold bedsit. Without doubt, I had struck gold and was invited to stay in the guest bedroom any time I wished, providing I read the family their favourite poems from time to time. It was an odd arrangement but I willingly obliged. My hours of voice and verse classes at Brufords had paid dividends, for I now had a cosy home in Penarth and a girlfriend who idolized me thrown in. 'Daddy darling' of managerial status, would sit in the large living room in front of me with his chequebook open and ask 'mummy dear' how much she wanted for that new washing machine she had spotted in the Cardiff House of Fraser. The cheque was written with a flourish and I was duly impressed; 'daddy darling' was very good at that.

Like a madman I asked Jill to marry me and she agreed. Gifts from the two families came flooding in from every quarter. I read more poetry and the family looked with adoration upon their intended son-in-law. I could not afford an engagement ring however and 'daddy darling' was not going to finance that little item. Best to wait until I was in work and I felt certain there would be plenty of that speeding my way once I finished college in the summer.

I thought it wise to bring together the two lots of parents in order that friendships could be struck up and it would give 'mummy dear' a chance to have a good natter about weddings. We all arranged to meet in a pub at some half-way point between Cardiff and Aberystwyth. I was slightly worried to say the least. Firstly, everything was galloping at a breakneck speed and Jill's family was almost naming the church and starting their walk up the aisle. Secondly, my parents did not, in any way, resemble 'mummy dear' and 'daddy darling' – both couples were from opposite ends of the social spectrum, or appeared to be. We passed an hour or two in the pub amicably enough, with Jill and me stargazing at each other and both sets of parents struggling to find some common ground. When I asked my father, some days later, what he thought of 'daddy darling', he responded with his usual dry Welsh wit. "I noticed when it was time to pay for the drinks at the bar, his elbow came up but his hand only went halfway towards his wallet!" My family would be laughing at that line for years to come.

The engagement rumbled on for the next six months.

***

Almost as a final gesture of defiance to our passing early years, although more relevantly to our three years of study, Geraint Morris, our friend from the Cardiff college had a plan. He asked a few of us boys home for tea; it was a chance to meet his mum and dad and an opportunity for him to show us where his early years were spent in Gwaelod y Garth. Six miles north of Cardiff, his house lay at the foot of a mountain called 'Garth Hill' or 'Mynydd y Garth' in Welsh. From its summit you can see for miles around and lying adjacent to the mountain is the Taff Vale with the village of Pentyrch on one side. The Garth has gained fame in recent years by being the subject of the film, *The Englishman Who Went Up a Hill But Came Down a Mountain* (1995). The film, starring Hugh Grant, was directed by Christopher Monger, a native of nearby Taffs Well and the story, which came from his grandfather, although fictional and not filmed on the Garth, was about the inhabitants of a Welsh village claiming their mountain was indeed a mountain and was not a hill, as it was of the required, official minimum height of 1,000 feet.

The film was released in 1995 but, in 1963, Geraint had other plans for the Garth. He supplied us all with a tin tray and instructed us to follow him up the mountain. It was a fair climb but from the summit we had a stunning view of Cardiff and its docks on one side and the Taff Vale to the other. Once we had reached the top, we lazed in the sunshine, lay on our backs in the heather and looked up at the clear blue sky. Then it was all bums on trays as we slid, at great speed down the Garth, shouting and whooping like kids just out of school. Bumping

Newspapers
proclaim the
nightly bombing
of Cardiff
By kind permission of
Media Wales and Cardiff
Central Library

There was humour in
those dark days of war
© *Punch* magazine

"*By the way, did you remember to feed the canary?*"

The aftermath of a three-night blitz on Swansea in early 1941
By kind permission of Swansea City Council Archives

Our Mum and Dad in the 1930s

Scamps one and all: me (sitting right) with my pals

Pontrhydyfen – a south Wales mining
village from where came a wealth of talent

A highly cherished autograph
from the early 1950s

Now demolished,
miners' cottages
in Pontrhydyfen
– split by
a road. My
grandmother's
cottage is on the
left and the right.

The book of
magic that
started it all

In my scout camp in the 1950s, promising to do my best for Queen and country.
Me (back row, right) next to my scoutmaster.

Walter Lewis, town thespian and a magician to admire

By kind permission of the Lewis family

I even rehearsed the magic outside; note the tails and baggy trousers

The college prospectus with principal, Rose Bruford

By kind permission of Special Collections at the Rose Bruford College of Theatre and Performance

THE ROSE BRUFORD
TRAINING COLLEGE
OF
SPEECH AND DRAMA
(Recognised by the Ministry of Education)
LAMORBEY PARK . SIDCUP . KENT
Telephone : FOOtscray 3024-5

The cast from *The Happiest Days...* Me in glasses (at the back), sister Jean bottom left corner.

The Bruford first year students in 1960, all being over-dramatic. Me, top right in a dark jacket.

By kind permission of Bernard Holly and Special Collections at the Rose Bruford College of Theatre and Performance

Rose Bruford with the wonderful actress and college patron, Dame Sybil Thorndike

By kind permission of Special Collections at the Rose Bruford College of Theatre and Performance

Cardiff Castle housed the music and drama college in the early 1960s

Photograph courtesy of Mike Roberts

Principal, Dr Raymond Edwards commemorated in a portrait by artist, John Elwyn

By kind permission of Royal Welsh College of Music and Drama, Cardiff

The late Peter Palmer (right), my voice tutor in Sidcup and Cardiff in 1960–3

By kind permission of Fiona Palmer

A student production of *The Tinker* in 1963. Me sitting centre, Geraint Morris to the right.

My three-minute moment of magic on BBC television surpassed my dancing skills
© BBC Wales

Prompter, messenger and dispatch rider in *Antigone*

The late Geraint Morris, a generous friend who kick-started my career. A talented television producer of such programmes as *Z Cars*; *Softly, Softly*; *The Onedin Line* and *Casualty*

Courtesy of Siân Morris

"RING OUT AN ALIBI".   Episode 6.

by

EYNON EVANS.

PRODUCED BY: ARTHUR WILLIAMS.

Crew.	ONE.
Technical Manager.	TONY ESCOTT
A.T.M.	GEOFF ALFORD
Sound Supervisor.	GRAHAM GAMBLES
Production Assistant.	GERAINT MORRIS
Senior Cameraman.	DAVID JONES
Asst. Floor Manager.	DAVID LLOYD
Vision Mixer.	MEIRION MAINWARING
Design.	COLIN SHAW
Make-up Supervisor.	JUDY TARLING
Wardrobe Supervisor.	COLLEEN O'BRIEN
Secretary.	GILLIAN GORE

For the first time, I am part of a television studio crew on *Ring Out an Alibi*

Courtesy of BBC Wales

END OF TELECINE 1.

Who wrote all those camera directions? I was yet to learn.

Courtesy of BBC Wales

4. Cam 1A.	As Bowen puts up hand to knock door m.s.Living Room. Elinor comes out of lounge & crosses to front door.	SCENE 2. THE LIVI THE DOOR KNOCKER IS ALSO IS BULLER'S B.
5. Cam 3A.	As door is opened 2s. Bowen/Elinor, favour Bowen.	ELINOR HURRIES TO TO ADMIT THE SERGE
6. Cam 2A.	2s at front door. Elinor/Bowen,fav. Elinor.	BOWEN: Mrs. Cha
3A-3B trap, fairly fast.		
7. Cam 1A.	As Sgt.enters 2s Elinor/Bowen. They	ELINOR: Come in, been expecting yo

Proud Scot, James Buchan, who rescued Grampian Television and offered me a job in 1966

Exterior of Grampian Television – an artist's impression. Now long demolished.
By kind permission of Eileen Doris Bremner

Once an agricultural hall in the middle of Norwich, but in 1966 Anglia House was home of Anglia Television
By kind permission of ITV Anglia

Room for nearly two thousand 'bums on seats' – the Odeon Cinema in Balham SW12
By kind permission of Dusashen

Tales of the Unexpected – an identifiable programme in its day
By kind permission of ITV Anglia

How many of us remember the revolving knight on a horse? Anglia TV's logo.
By kind permission of ITV Anglia

3.33 Rumblie Jumblie
RONALD SAWDON
Join Ronald and all his young friends in the Rumblie Jumblie room.
DIRECTOR DAVID LLOYD
Grampian Television Production

A credit for my indoctrination into directing one of my first television programmes

The Aberdeen and Highland audiences in full flow at *Calum's Céilidh*
By kind permission of Eddie Joffe

Me in a kilt with presenter and entertainer, Calum Kennedy and director, Tony Bacon

The *Bothy Nichts* programme with me in a tub!

Production assistant Eileen, director Alan Wallace, and me pulling a gun – or so it seems
By kind permission of Eileen Doris Bremner

The gracious and multitalented James Spankie playing the pipes on *Ye Banks and Braes*
By kind permission of James Spankie

My friend and partner in studio floor managing, the late Alan Franchi catching a salmon on the River Dee . Also, Alan's wife and broadcaster, Jane Franchi
By kind permission of Jane Franchi

I play the dotty vicar in *The Black Sheep of the Family* for the Grampian TV drama club

HTV Wales logo and the old Pontcanna studios
Courtesy of ITV Wales / National Library of Wales

Lord Harlech and the Harlech logo
Courtesy of ITV Wales / National Library of Wales

Managing the studio floor (I hope!) at Grampian Television in 1967

Keeping the audience sweet and applauding for HTV's *Sion a Siân* in 1972

Rehearsing Grampian's programme for young people

Studio crew on Grampian's *Bothy Nichts*

Paul Starling interviews
Neil Kinnock MP during
the miners' strike

Mike Lloyd-Williams
prepares to go on air

Wales at Six logo

I say something
amusing to HRH The
Prince of Wales

Inheritors studio set with
Robert Uquart and Peter
Egan

Courtesy of ITV Wales / National Library
of Wales

Mike Lloyd-Williams and
David Bellin on the *Report
Wales* news set

Courtesy of Ron Lewis

Ron Lewis interviewing for
Wales at Six

Courtesy of Ron Lewis

and thumping through the heather and soft grass at breakneck speed, we were kids again or maybe kids for the last time. We were in our own worlds, with the wind buffeting our faces. It was a good place to be. My Wales, I could see it beneath me as if I were flying and soaring like a great bird over the Welsh countryside. My mind flooded with thoughts of my childhood in Aberystwyth, with the wild winds blowing in my face as we sledged down hills in winter and climbed trees and ran through fields in summer and played on the beach for hours, teasing the tides and damming the streams and splashing our ankles in the rock pools. My world was full of the joys of childhood as I slid hell-for-leather over bracken and gravel and saw my years in college racing up to meet me and then... a jolting halt as we slid off our tin trays and rolled over and over like rolling pins and lay on our backs for the second time that afternoon, and looked up at the sky and laughed... and laughed. And then the laughing subsided as reality and the realisation that we were glad to be there, at that moment, with each other, but now had to justify our training. We all had something to prove to the world. Our future would now be guided by what little talent and skill we possessed but it was up to each one of us to face the future bravely. That joyous slide down the Garth defined something. It symbolised the end of one way of life for another. Rehearsals were over; time to put away childish things and take our first tentative step into the adult world of work, and this time there would be no turning back.

***

College days were now over and it was down to the grim reality of job hunting. The letters poured out of my bedsit, letters of application to every theatre company in the country, but I was too late. Contracts had already been signed months earlier. Actors had been booked until Christmas and beyond. I lay on my bed and looked across at the wall. I was broke and needed money to live and pay the rent. After a restless night I decided to call the Welsh Theatre Company based in Cardiff. The company was on my doorstep. They called me for an audition and by lunchtime I had been offered a job and was given a three-month contract of employment. I knew it, I was going to be one of the lucky ones. Straight out of drama college and into a job. I was now a professional actor. I rang home and I rang Jill to tell her my good fortune. Moving from Kent to Cardiff had been the wisest thing to do. I felt so proud and 'mummy dear' and 'daddy darling' asked me to read some poetry before they retired to bed.

***

For me, the hard graft of rehearsals started in an old church hall in Islington. There were two plays to be performed across Wales, making good theatre available to people in rural areas with subsidised coaches to bring people from the countryside to their nearest town to see a professionally performed play. I was lucky to be given parts in both plays. *Antigone* by Jean Anouilh was a Greek classic but set within a contemporary place. Produced originally in Paris in 1942, it was about the state versus the individual – an irreconcilable clash, when France was part of Hitler's Europe. Our second play, *The Keep* by Gwyn Thomas, was about a south Wales family who lived in a precarious unity held together by the memory of a brilliant and creative mother.

I was now a professional actor and an assistant stage manager and the two jobs combined were labour intensive and backbreaking. The sets were enormous and as heavy as lead and it took every scrap of energy we possessed to load and unload from furniture lorry to the stages of theatres in twelve Welsh towns. It took four of us to raise the *Antigone* ceiling piece and we were loading and unloading it from one play to the next every few nights across Wales, together with lighting batons and heavy rostra, baskets, boxes, lighting consoles, make-up mirrors and tables. That was just for *Antigone*. *The Keep* had three times the amount. A heavily decorated living room with a porchway beyond and a hundred props from ashtrays to coal scuttles, china dogs, Bibles, paintings, tables and chairs. On top of all this work, we needed to keep an eye on the parts we were playing. We were covered in dirt and sweat most days, and hardly had the energy to walk on stage let alone act the part. We stayed in small hotels and slept like tired dogs, too exhausted to undress but with just enough strength left to fall onto the bed, lifeless and filthy on top of the bedclothes and sleep solidly until morning. We woke with every limb aching and filled our bodies with a breakfast that would have to last the day – there was little time to eat. Bruford's prophetic words would echo through my brain. "You will learn to suffer for your art. The theatre owes you nothing."

In London, during rehearsals, I was staying in digs in Parliament Hill Fields and breakfast came with the rent for the bed. There was no money in my pocket for anything else to eat then and I would return to the digs and smell the food being prepared for some German students downstairs and my tummy would complain until sleep took over.

One morning in north Wales I blew, and flew off the handle. I turned to my friends, the deputy stage managers who were sharing the bedroom with me and, in a raging temper, I yelled, "IT'S ALRIGHT FOR THOSE F*****G MANAGERS IN CARDIFF SHARPENING THEIR BLOODY PENCILS, LOOKING AT A F*****G MAP AND DECIDING WHERE WE SHOULD GO TO NEXT. THEY ARE JUST FINE AND DANDY LIVING IN THEIR F*****G POSH HOUSES IN BLOODY CYNCOED... THEY HAVE NO IDEA WHAT..."

We all looked at each other, faces ragged and torn, and the eczema on my hands bloodying the bedclothes. We all smiled and fell about laughing like mad fools. We would often find ourselves on a stage, bearing the weight of the ceiling piece and our arms collapsing with tiredness, muscles bulging, sweat running down our faces and my colleague Tony looking at me over his glasses with signs of enormous strain on his face saying, "Hey Superman, what was that you said about those men sharpening their bloody pencils?" Laughter took over as the ceiling piece became heavier and we found ourselves being slowly crushed under its weight.

Setting and dressing the stage one day in readiness for a performance of *The Keep*, I hung the overcoats and jackets on the hooks in the porch. The porch was clearly visible to the audience. I hung the overcoats in no particular way and I was immediately stopped by one of the deputy stage managers. As it happened I had not hung them as per the continuity photograph that had been taken when the set was initially installed.

"Does it matter, they are only coats and jackets?" I retorted.

"David, do it and do it now," came his reply.

"I don't see the point: a waste of time. I have enough to do," I argued back.

The deputy stage manager moved so fast I could hardly register his speed. He flung me back on the settee and his face, full of anger, came within an inch of mine.

"Under my watch sonny boy, you set this stage exactly as it was set the first time, right down to the last tintack. You call yourself a professional theatre man, well let me tell you something and you listen good and hard. There are people around here struggling to make these performances work and you come in here expecting it all to happen around you. Well, let me tell you something, clever boy. You will never get anywhere in this business, in films, theatre or television without hard slog and making sure everything is 100 per cent right on this stage for the actors who will be using it in five hours from now. DO YOU GET MY DRIFT OR DO I HAVE TO CLOUT YOU ROUND THE HEAD WITH THE MESSAGE?"

He was fuming and front-of-house people had come into the auditorium to see what all the commotion was about. He rose from the settee and looked down on me, his voice lowered in pitch.

"Sort it out now, please."

I had learned Rose Bruford's lesson the hard way.

The stages for the rest of the run were always set as the director, designer, stage manager and actors would wish them. Ashtrays had sand in the bottom so that cigarettes could be extinguished quickly. Drinks were diluted and spirit bottles had suitable colouring in them. Furniture and props were always in the right place: newspapers, books, spills for lighting a pipe, carpets stuck down with two-sided gaffer tape, china dogs, cutlery, fenders and companion sets. Every prop that was handled was set precisely; even a box of matches would have a match protruding from the drawer for ease of handling. I was beginning to understand the difference between professional and amateur, between drama college and real theatre.

***

It was a tour of some magnitude, visiting twelve theatres around Wales. It was hard, hard work, stage managing and playing parts, but wonderful to be with professional actors and watch them work. In Cardiff's New Theatre, the season climaxed with two additional plays, *War and Peace*, in which I rushed on stage as a Napoleonic soldier and was immediately caught in the crossfire of gunshots and had to lie on stage motionless as a corpse for 15 minutes, and *Semi-Detached*, on which I was an assistant stage manager. The days were long and arduous with technical runs and dress runs, and most of my few sleeping hours spent on the dressing room floor. It's surprising how comfortable a hard floor can be when you are dog-tired from painting and changing sets and carrying rostra all day from eight in the morning to midnight.

I shouted a prompt to 1960s film star, Paul Massie, when he didn't want a prompt. I am sure he had never paused in that particular spot in the script during rehearsal but, on stage, during performance, he did and my voice belted out the words across the New Theatre stage. When he strode off stage, his temper was at boiling point.

"I DID NOT REQUIRE THAT PROMPT," he yelled and rushed off into his star dressing room furious with that incompetent assistant stage manager. My apology did not improve matters one iota but one other thing I do remember from that night was hearing of President Kennedy's assassination: 22 November 1963.

At last, the season drew to a close and my contract came to an end. It had all been a wonderful experience. Hard slog, yes, and lessons learned the hard way. I went to Penarth to see Jill and her parents. Things had changed. I was now sleeping in the attic and there was a distinct shortage of poetry-reading requests. My frugal salary in the theatre had not impressed 'mummy dear' and 'daddy darling' and the nomadic existence I had been leading was not one they wanted for their daughter. I had somehow managed to buy an engagement ring on hire-purchase some weeks earlier, but now it was waiting for me to collect on top of the neat pile of bed sheets, towels and salad servers that had been given us for our engagement. It was time to call it a day. The family were pretending to be something else; their snobbery had not impressed my family, and any feelings I had for Jill were not being reciprocated. To say I was not upset would be telling an untruth, but tomorrow was another day and soon I would be going home for Christmas and all thoughts of Jill would be buried beneath all the festive celebrations.

CHAPTER 6

The Running Man

IT WAS CHRISTMAS 1963 and I was broke. The money I had earned in the theatre had been stretched to the very limit. It was not as if I had been partying it away, either. Even from the beginning, there had been no money for parties or drinking because we literally had no time for such luxuries. I sold the engagement ring to Grimwade's, a shop for second-hand goods in Cardiff. I needed the cash badly, for I owed two weeks' rent. The little money I had went on day-to-day survival and if I was going home for Christmas, remedial action would have to be taken. The Post Office in Cardiff was seeking people to help with the Christmas rush and I jumped at the opportunity. I was now one of a whole band of men who were in similar circumstances, some more desperate than others. I took heart. John, one of my friends from the Cardiff college, was in a similar position and he too had signed on for work in the Western Avenue sorting office. It was hardly an office but a large factory floor full of mail bags, noise and dust, with Post Office lorries driving in loaded with thousands of bulging sacks. Teams of us were deployed to unload the mail and distribute it to its correct place on the floor. Envelopes were tossed into rows of little open-ended boxes and parcels and packages were hurled into other waiting sacks. Sacks were kept for broken parcels that never reached their destination. It was an unbearably cold place, full of noise and diesel fumes.

The experience dispelled all the myths of Christmas with a red-cheeked Father Christmas loading his sleigh. This was labour intensive, hard graft and our foreman was an unsmiling, sour individual who took delight in giving us more hard labour whenever it seemed we were taking a breather. He would come round with our pay packets and pretend mine was missing, or drop it to the floor and wait for me to pick it up. There was one ten-minute tea break mid-morning when we ate our own sandwiches and drank our own tea. Lunch was one hour and came from the paper bag I had prepared the night before. We finished work at six in the evening and night shifts would then take over. This was chain gang treatment without the end-of-the-day delight of walking on stage and performing. John and I would study the other workers; some of them looked so desperately thin and worn. These were the city underdogs who scratched a living from pillar to post and lived in their own world of need. The days were cold with ice and bitter winds, and my walk across Llandaff Fields at 6 a.m. every morning to reach the sorting depot was done purely and simply for the money. The walk, however, was becoming more laboured. My asthma was getting worse and I developed bronchitis. My hands were torn to shreds by handling the sacks, which brought on my eczema and my skin was constantly itching and bleeding. The dust from the depot filled my lungs and that aggravated my asthma. All in all, I was in a mess, and I was glad to see the end of the job. I had one day left to buy Christmas presents before catching the bus home and collapsing with severe bronchitis over the Christmas period. Today, I have the deepest respect for postal workers but doubtless their working conditions have changed for the better. As for the old sorting depot on Western Avenue in Cardiff: it is now a very large Tesco.

***

Christmas came and went but I was still not fit enough to return to the city. I stayed home and enjoyed the creature comforts. I returned to south Wales and took a job with a wholesale fruit and vegetable business in the Cardiff fruit market, which occupied a large area in the lower part of the city – anything to improve my monetary situation. I was invited to stay with relatives for a short while, which was another saving. From 6.30 a.m. onwards, I loaded fruit and vegetables onto lorries and worked in a warehouse. My financial situation marginally improved; I thanked my aunt and moved to a bedsit on the western side of the city.

I wrote to a Cardiff BBC producer who was casting for a light entertainment show in Welsh. At the same time, I noticed a fellow student from Brufords was performing in the New Theatre. Elizabeth was a professional dancer in the chorus line and I decided to make contact.

"Do you have a dance partner?" the BBC enquired.

"Of course," was my stalwart reply.

"Come for an audition next Wednesday at 2.30 and bring your music on a tape or record."

I was wild with excitement. At last a chance. I would contact Liz at the New Theatre and we would dance for the BBC like Fred Astaire and Ginger Rogers.

Liz was delighted with an opportunity to do some telly. She quickly learned I was no dancer. To the song, 'We're a Couple of Swells', we rehearsed furiously for the rest of the week and into the next. I could not get it right as hard as I tried. Elizabeth was superb. She had choreographed the routine and taught me the steps but remembering them in the right order was an impossible task. I was no hoofer but Elizabeth did all she humanly could to drill the routine into my brain. If my brain had it, my feet didn't and we faced an uncertain audition. When the day dawned, we arrived at the studio and the producer, Meredydd Evans and his production assistant, complete with clipboard and stopwatch, sat behind a table and waited to be entertained. I fear my feet developed a life of their own. We started the routine well enough, with Elizabeth and I dancing like real troupers, but then my memory became something resembling scrambled egg and my feet took me one way and Elizabeth went the other. As hard as I tried to correct it, the problem became exacerbated by even more mistakes. I tried to catch up and danced the remainder of the routine like an out-of-synch film where the sound does not match the picture. I brought shame on both of us. There was a pause as the producer and his PA muttered something under their breath and scribbled some notes on the clipboard. They finally looked up and Mr Evans smiled then spoke.

"Well done both. Thank you very much. Now then, Elizabeth, I could see you gave a very polished performance. You are obviously a professional dancer are you not?"

Elizabeth nodded.

"I thought so. Now then, David." He looked at me squarely in the eye and in the kindest of voices said, "Is there anything else that you can do on this show? I get the distinct feeling that dancing is not your forte; would I be right?"

I nodded ashamedly and replied with one word, "Magic".

He looked at his PA and then at me and asked for some clarification.

"I do magic," I replied. I am a magician, I have been a man of magic for years. I can do a conjuring show."

His eyes lit up and he seemed surprised.

"Wonderful. A man of magic. Come around to my office for an audition in a week's time. OK?"

I do not recall Elizabeth's solo performance but I was given a three-minute spot on a Welsh light entertainment show called, *Hip Hip Hwrê* which went out early on Saturday evenings in Wales. I recall performing the magic to some Mantovani music. Three years in drama college learning to act, and I end up doing a three-minute magic show on television, which is what I was doing before I went to college. I could make no sense of it. I rushed home to Aberystwyth on Saturday morning to watch the programme that evening with my family. A small television picture, in glorious black and white, with me dressed in a dark suit, white shirt, dickey bow and a crooked smile.

***

There was something about bedsits in the 1960s that sent me into stagnation mode. A single bed, with a bedside table and an old-fashioned table lamp. Carpet laid over lino. There was a small table for writing and eating and a rather uncomfortable granny chair placed alongside a gas fire that was fed off a shilling meter. There were one or two wall cupboards and usually some hideous-looking wallpaper and cracks in the ceiling. In the wallpaper, if I gazed at it long enough, I could make out a man running. There he was running with large strides across my wall – no bodily detail but a very good outline. I would lie on my bed, propped up against the pillow and see the running man as large as life.

The lady behind the counter in the Employment Office was sympathetic when she put me on the dole. I filled out the forms and handed them back.

"Thank you love. Filled them out correctly? Good. Any work yet love?"

I shook my head.

"OK, love. Come back on Tuesday for your money."

Tuesday. That was three whole days away. I had £2 left to my name; could I make it stretch? Tuesday nights were special: I would use a little of my dole money to visit an Indian restaurant in Cardiff – the first of its kind. Chicken off-the-bone and mushroom curry with boiled rice and spices to burn my palate. What a treat that was.

***

The Welsh Theatre Company made contact to tell me the BBC wanted them to do *Antigone* on the radio. Would I be prepared to play my part of the messenger? "I will just check my diary," I recall saying, trying to give the impression I was a busy working actor. I agreed to take the part for a radio fee which was not extortionate but would pay for a few more chicken off-the-bone and mushroom curries.

***

75

The long process of recording a radio play was now over and it was back to the dole office.

"Had any parts love?"

"No, 'fraid not," I replied, deciding to keep my BBC fee a big secret.

Two other jobs for the BBC followed, one involved holding a spear in a Welsh television play set during the Roman conquest. I had a stinking cold but the money was reasonable. The second job was totally different to anything I had done in the past. Would I do an item please for *Good Morning Wales*? – a morning radio show for the BBC. I could collect a portable tape recorder from the BBC sound studios in Park Place and go down to the steelworks early on the following morning to conduct some interviews with steelworkers who were threatening strike action. I completed the job and rushed the tapes to the BBC studio where the producer was busy at work editing and assembling the programme. I rushed home to the bedsit and caught the item being transmitted at 8.15 that same morning.

"Once again, steelworkers in north and south Wales are threatening strike action and management and the Government are already beginning to count the cost of previous disruption. With another strike looming in the steel industry, we went down to East Moors in Cardiff this morning to catch the night shift coming off duty. David Lloyd reports."

"YES, YES, YES," I shouted, thrashing my fist into the air. "You are a big, beautiful man David Lloyd and you sounded bloody wonderful. A report on *Good Morning Wales*, and the whole of Wales heard you." I rang Mum and Dad and they were over the moon. Their phone at home did not stop ringing with friends and neighbours, saying they had heard me on the wireless. Had any of my ex-teachers heard it? Any of my old friends? The vicar? The curate? Rose Bruford? I cared not. I slept the rest of that morning, a happy and contented man.

Even the lady in the dole office was looking brighter than usual. Maybe she had heard my report on the wireless.

"Any parts love?" she said with a smile.

"No," I replied, "Not exactly parts," said I with a grin.

She moved on to her next client. She had obviously not listened to *Good Morning Wales* that day. Was I witnessing a change of direction in my career perhaps? Was I destined to become a reporter on the radio? I seemed to be quite good at it. Maybe the BBC would ask me again. Suffice to say, they did not and that was the end of my journalistic career. The phone went silent and the post dried up.

***

My brain was clogged with anxiety as days spread into weeks. My spirits were at an all-time low and by degrees I could feel myself slowing up. I was no longer running like the man on my wallpaper: he was running across the wall in leaps and bounds and I was standing in porridge. A letter from my father came in the morning post.

Dear David

I am enclosing a small cheque for you, so go careful. Remember to see the public assistance officer. Something is bound to turn up sooner or later. You must have patience. By the way, have you sent to the BBC in London for an application form. Remember they have selections in January. If there are any stage management jobs going in any theatre in any part of the country, you must apply. I would not bank on staying in Cardiff if you can get some work elsewhere. What about your coat – you should have it down there in this cold weather.

If you feel fed-up, come back home until February. You can apply for jobs David quite as easily from here. There is no need to panic. Give us a ring one evening.

Love

Dad

PS: Always keep your dignity and when possible go to church.

I still have that letter and cherish it to this day.

***

The phone rang downstairs. The landlady's voice cried out my name. I leapt down the stairs, two at a time.

"Is that you young Lloyd?"

"It is. Who's that?"

"Jack." (Jack being Geraint Morris from the Cardiff college. We always called him Jack, after his role of Jack Chesney in the college production of *Charley's Aunt.*)

"Jack, lovely man, how are you?"

"Fine. Fine."

"What are you up to?"

"Listen now bachgen." (boy, in Welsh)

"I'm all ears Jack. What are you up to these days?"

"Listen, will you. What are YOU up to these days is more to the point?"

I considered my answer carefully. I did not want to give him the impression that I was dying a slow death in a Cardiff bedsit.

"Well, I've been quite busy Jack. A few bit parts here and there. A piece for *Good Morning Wales* and a tour with the Welsh Theatre Company."

"Listen Lloyd. I am now a PA in the BBC in Cardiff working on a forthcoming television drama serial and I need an assistant on the studio floor. Are you interested? We start rehearsals in two weeks in the church hall. You would have to come in and meet the producer on Monday morning – just for an informal chat. You would be on contract for three months. What do you think?"

I thought it through.

"Will there be any acting involved Jack because as you know I am really a professional actor," said I, being a total idiot.

"No, man. This is not an acting job I am offering you. This is an assistant floor manager's job, assisting me in rehearsals and on the studio floor. I told Arthur Williams, the producer, you might be the boy for the job."

Yet again, I idiotically played hard to get and stumbled my way through a few lame excuses.

"Look Dave boy, I have to rush now. Think about it over the weekend and call me back on Monday morning at ten." He rang off.

I thought through my situation... You are broke, Lloyd, with five shillings between you and the workhouse and that has to last till Tuesday. There are no theatre jobs coming your way and you are on the dole. Is this the reason you left home and went through all that training? To be sitting here in a dump of a room in the middle of Cardiff with no hope and no prospects. As hard as I tried to find alternative arguments for defending my cause to remain an actor, I could find none. The job on offer was for a mere three months but it would give me an important income and help rebuild my resources for seeking future jobs in the theatre.

I rang Jack on Monday morning and confirmed with a positive response. "When do I start Jack?" "Good boy!" he shouted in his inimitable style. "Come to the office in an hour Dave and meet the producer."

I failed to notice the running man that morning. I walked down Cathedral Road with a skip in my step. It was a bright autumn morning and I was excited and thrilled about starting something completely different. What would come next? My adventure had only just begun.

CHAPTER 7

Life on the Floor

I was mesmerized, stunned, captivated.

For the third time in my young life, I walked into Studio A at the BBC Television headquarters in Cardiff. This time, in April 1964, a performance was not required of me and I stood there in the silence, rooted to the spot, disbelieving my situation and gazing in astonishment at the fabricated world I had entered. The studios, once an old chapel in the Broadway area of the city, no longer looked like a chapel on the inside. One side of the studio was the interior of a coal mine: black as black, complete with wooden pit props holding up the tunnel. There was a Davy lamp lightly burning, pickaxes and shovels and tramcars loaded with coal standing silent on a railway track. I could almost breathe the coal dust, smell the coal and feel the claustrophobia of life underground. Opposite this incredible display was a small kitchenette with a Welsh dresser laden with china and in the centre a table with chairs. There was a high mantelpiece surrounding a warm glowing fire and everything about this cosy place, lit dimly with a few oil lamps, suggested a family had just vacated it. At one end of the studio, there was a street with shop fronts, a pavement and an old gas lamp. Everything about it looked so real. There were First World War posters on the brick wall and a newspaper stand. At the opposite end, a court of law, complete with judge's chair and desk. There were benches for the prosecution and defence, plus collections of learned books and papers. I had entered the make-believe world of television drama and what looked so realistic to the eye of the camera was, in fact, constructed from polystyrene and cleverly painted canvas on wooden frames held up by stage weights and braces. The designer, a certain Mr Julian Williams from Aberystwyth, had designed this set so realistically and with such finesse that I just stood there trying to take it all in: The large cameras on their hydraulic bases, lifeless and unmanned, and on the floor, miles of black cable and two large platforms on wheels, carried microphones on arms that were extended to pick up the voices of the actors. The ceiling, or the grid, as it was called, carried a conglomeration of lamps, all suspended on a maze of overhead scaffold which extended from one end of the studio to the other. The lamps were blazing away, lighting the sets with such a density of light that I could barely look at them. This was my first visit to a television studio as a freelance assistant floor manager working on a television drama, and I was spellbound with excitement.

***

BBC Television in Wales in the early 1960s was an exciting place to be with an adventurous mix of programmes led by executive controller, Alun Oldfield-Davies, and a line-up of some distinguished producers. The cornerstone of what was to become BBC Cymru/Wales was most certainly cast by pioneers like Selwyn Roderick and drama producers, D.J. Thomas and Dafydd Gruffydd – two men prolific in their drama output. Drama series like *Moulded in Earth*, *The House Under the Water*, and *How Green Was My Valley* brought home to the viewers the realisation that the BBC in Wales could be as ambitious and effective in television drama as any on the English network. In fact, drama from Wales became a regular monthly event in the English schedules with actors like Emrys James, Henley Thomas, Philip Madoc and Windsor Davies becoming household names and familiar faces.

The news and sport came from a building in Stacey Road, a mere stone's throw away from the church. This was the home of *Heddiw* (Today) fronted by a man, the very embodiment of a thoroughbred Welshman, named Owen Edwards who looked clean-cut and appealingly good on camera and was a highly intelligent investigative Welsh journalist. The wonderful thing about *Heddiw* was that it was transmitted to the Midlands live every lunchtime and was not seen in Wales until that evening. It begged the question of how many Welsh viewers there were in the Midlands watching the programme, apart from those who were watching out of sheer linguistic curiosity. Owen was as popular in Telford as he was in Aberystwyth, which is where he was born and lived for the early part of his life. Also from that studio came *Wales Today*, edited by Alan Protheroe and featuring the news readers, Brian Hoey, John Darran and occasionally, Ronnie Williams. John was a Cardiff solicitor by day and a newsreader at night.

***

I would be assisting Geraint in a murder drama serial called, *Ring Out an Alibi* written by Eynon Evans, who was no stranger to me as we had been together in *The Keep* at the New Theatre. My first job was to 'tape' the rehearsal room floor. After the initial read-through, which all actors dread, they rehearsed with the director on a hired church hall floor. The sets were still being built elsewhere in Cardiff but they existed on a studio floor plan, worked out to scale by a designer. Every set, including the living room, the kitchen and stairways, the windows and doors, the chief inspector's office and the belfry were all created for rehearsal by marking them out with coloured tape on the church hall floor. The living room was denoted with red sticky-backed tape and the kitchenette with yellow. The bedrooms upstairs were indicated with green tape and overlapped the downstairs rooms, the belfry in one corner, the chief inspector's in another. One ended up with a church hall floor unrecognisable to any stranger entering; a mass of meaningless, crisscross, vertical and horizontal coloured tapes all shooting off in different directions. You will have guessed correctly if I were to say I messed it all up! When Arthur Williams, our esteemed producer, turned up the day before rehearsals to check things out, the hallway was twice as big as it should have been and in the living room you would not have swung a cat. I apologised to Geraint, who in turn apologised to Arthur. We re-laid it all again that evening. Geraint explained how to go about it and made the job look so simple. As for furniture and simple props, we made do with anything that came to hand. Tables and chairs and other bric-a-brac came from wherever we could find them. It's surprising how old church halls yielded up a plentiful supply of fixtures and fittings. If there were props to be handled by the actors, every effort was made to find them something similar for rehearsals.

The props department back at the studios would get a list of our requirements and made sure they were delivered to the hall on time, including coffee and tea for the thirsting actors with biscuits to hand.

The difference between working at the BBC and in the theatre was that in television in those days there were whole departments of people to supply you with the necessary back-up; from prop men to painters, designers and electricians. And so rehearsals would start with the producer and cast discussing individual parts and the plot. Arthur would rehearse tirelessly with them, moving them to different positions on the floor and looking through a small viewfinder to make sure he could get the shots he wanted. At early rehearsals, actors would read their parts off the script but, as the week progressed, lines were committed to memory. Geraint would make copious notes and hand prop requirements to me. I was the dogsbody, running all over the hall or into town to fetch or purchase anything the episode would require. I looked after actors and rehearsed their lines with them, transported them in hired vehicles and

I made sure they knew what times they were needed by the producer and arranged costume fittings and photo calls for them.

During the technical run at the end of the week, problems would be discussed and ironed out with the heads of the technical departments and the actors, usually in full flow, would be stopped in their tracks while Arthur discussed the lighting with the lighting director or the framing of the camera shots with the senior cameraman.

The studio day arrived and the actors and crew got to see the real sets for the first time. With the lighting plan worked out and all the lamps in their correct position, this was a feast for the eyes. Everything looked so real and the actors were impressed. For the first time, they would be able to walk through what looked like real doors, climb up stairs, open windows and handle props that were as real as could be. The day was set in tablets of stone. The best part of the day was spent rehearsing with cameras. What worked in the church hall might not necessarily work in the studio – although as near as possible it did, but there were always hitches that needed ironing out. Designer and carpenters were standing by in case any adjustment was needed to the scenery. We were all wearing 'cans'– an abbreviated word for earphones and we could hear Arthur 'up in the gallery' talking to Geraint on the floor and to the technical team. I would listen silently and intently, not yet fully understanding the technical or creative jargon.

"Geraint, can you ask Pat whether she can take up that position by the table please when she has that argument with Ray? Camera 3, are you able to frame her with a smudge of Watty's shoulder in left foreground?"

"Yes, Arthur, I think so, but we are getting a boom shadow across the door."

"OK, OK, Camera 2C, can you help out here please? OK, OK, that looks good. Shot 131 goes to Camera 2C – over shoulder Watty, favouring Pat. Camera 3, stay as you are on medium close-up Pat. Is that acceptable to you Tony?" Tony being the technical supervisor.

"Yes, we just have one lighting adjustment to make on the floor, Arthur."

"OK, OK, but make it quick, I'm pressing time. Sound, have you got that telephone ringing effect yet to cover shot 220?"

"Yes, Arthur, it's all ready to go."

"Good, thank you. Pat can now go to make-up. Tell her, Geraint, I will see her for notes in the canteen."

I had made up my mind. If I stayed in television, I would never consider being a director or producer. The very thought petrified me.

**

Time is our greatest enemy. Time is ticking by and there is a meal break coming up before the final run. Geraint is kept busy. Tempers have not frayed, yet. I am there at Geraint's shoulder should he need anything. I am running between studio, dressing rooms, prop room, wardrobe and make-up. The kitchen table needs re-dressing with a bowl of fruit and a tablecloth whilst they rehearse in the police station, and one of our actors wants me to fetch something from his dressing room. Wardrobe want permission to make an adjustment to Pat's coat on set and make-up thinks Ray needs dabbing down. Alan, the designer, wants our painter to clean up a corner of scenery. I hold them back. Geraint and Arthur are busy sorting out another problem, and so it goes on. Soon everyone has their turn and we break for a meal. At 8 p.m. we start recording the episode. No stops, no editing available, it has to be right first time. Geraint's voice can be heard across the studio floor.

"Stand-by everyone, studio doors locked Jim?" Jim nods in agreement.

"Everyone ready? Everyone happy and relaxed? Lovely actors ready?" The cast on set smile back and give him a thumbs up. Even those waiting to make their entrance behind the set, appear and smile.

"Studio ready, Arthur," Geraint says into the microphone at the end of the boom. He is aware of the tense situation developing on the studio floor but has a calming influence and an air of authority that commands respect from crew and artistes alike.

"David, stand-by with the Ampex clock. Start the clock." Ampex is the name of the machine, as large as a sideboard, in the technical area that is recording our episode on two-inch tape.

"Start the clock, David." I am holding the clock in front of a camera and the seconds tick by. One and a half minutes to go. I can feel the nervous tension up in the gallery through my earphones. Everyone is being put on stand-by mode. One minute to go. Geraint cracks a joke and people smile.

"Good luck everyone."

The heat in the studio is building and the electric fans have been switched off for recording. The back of my neck is wet with perspiration. Fifteen seconds and counting. This was rocket launch time.

"Roll Telecine 2," calls Gill Gore, the secretary sitting next to Arthur in the gallery.

"On titles for 25 seconds everyone."

The titles fronting the show look impressive. Arthur's voice comes through on the 'talk-back'.

"Stand-by to cue Pat through the door, stand-by Camera 1A, stand-by Boom A."

The secretary calls again.

"Coming out of titles in 10, 9, 8, 7, 6, 5, 4, 3, 2, 1."

Arthur, firmly and decisively, calls out, "Q PAT!" and Geraint gives her a cue. We are on air and before we know it the show moves forward, everyone working as a team, burning the adrenalin, on edge, working as a single entity. In one perfectly timed hour, we are rolling the end credits on a big wooden drum placed in front of a camera and the episode is 'in the can'. The recording must be spot-checked and we wait for clearance from the recording room. In five minutes, the all-clear is given, the show is over and everyone can relax and go across the road to the club for a drink. Arthur thanks everyone for their splendid work; he thanks Geraint and enquires how his new assistant did. Geraint replies with a cheeky smile that he thought I was reasonable for an Aberystwyth boy. Arthur laughs and says "Well done" and, to be perfectly honest with you, I loved the whole experience.

***

Episode five of *Ring Out an Alibi* and we learn that we have to go 'live'. Something has gone wrong in the programme scheduling between Cardiff and the network in London, which necessitates broadcasting a live episode in Wales. We rehearse until we are rock-solid in performance and then Geraint delivers me his blow.

"Do you know what a prompt button is young Lloyd?" he asks me on the day of our live transmission.

I shake my head, "I haven't a clue Mr Morris. What is a prompt button?" Geraint tells me that as we are going 'live' with the episode, one of my jobs will be to prompt the artistes should anyone of them dry. Sound department will give me a button attached to a rather long cable. If there is a 'dry', I press the button, keeping it depressed, yelling the prompt.

"What does that do?" I enquire, feeling my knees going weak and the colour draining from my face. Thoughts of my blunder with Mr Massie in the New Theatre fill my brain.

"It's simple," replies Geraint. "When you press the button, it knocks off all the sound coming from the studio and allows you to shout your prompt; not a soul out there in the wild, blue yonder will hear it. Simple, what?"

He has that cheeky smile on his face again and I think he is pulling my leg.

"You are pulling my leg of course, aren't you Jack?" I am

87

reverting to his name from *Charley's Aunt*, a rather endearing name which lovingly implies that a good old mate would never expect that from his close friend... or would he? Yes, he would. "There is no need to panic," Geraint replies, "Just keep your eyes fixed to the script and on the faces of the actors."

The studio's sound-proofed doors were sealed and red lights flashed to indicate we were going on air, no one would be allowed in or out during transmission. Wardrobe and make-up had set up a temporary base in a small corner to help actors with costume changes and powdering sweat off foreheads. This was a crucial time, everything had to work. I sensed a certain relief from the cast when they knew there was a prompt button being used. I stayed as close to the actors as I could. In that studio that night, we were all like a closely-knit family, dependent on each other to bring about a successful live transmission. There was no other job like this one. I was inexorably joined to the very fabric of that studio.

My finger hovered over that button for three-quarters of an hour. My eyes darted between the pages of the script and the faces of the actors. I practically knew, off by heart, every line. We were on the home run and everything was moving well. Cameras crept silently across the floor, the only sound being the lens turrets turning, And then, without warning, it happened. Watty, played by Ray Smith, was being interrogated by Detective Inspector Enoch Probert played by Eynon Evans – both men superb in their parts and very clever actors. Ray paused where there had never been a pause in the past and instinct told me he was searching for a line. His eye glanced up and my thumb slammed down on the button. I called the line, lifted my thumb back up from the button and Ray immediately picked up on the line. The whole event lasted less than three seconds. The show drew to a peaceful conclusion. Ray came up to me.

"Thanks Dave – perfect."

I struggled to say something.

"I was not sure..." Ray interjected. "You were spot-on buddy – my memory went blank."

Ray Smith went down in my book as being the ultimate professional. The moment had been so rapid that not even Arthur Williams had noticed. When the sound department informed him during the spot check that the prompt button had been used, he was amazed.

"Where, when?" he replied. I could not believe I had blocked the sound to every household television set in Wales... well... those households watching *Ring Out an Alibi*.

Arthur Williams bought me a drink in the club that night and said, "Well done Dave. Nicely done. I hadn't bloody noticed."

"He's not bad," said Jack, leaning against the bar with his beer and winking mischievously yet again. The end-of-series party was a wonderful affair.

***

My contract had been extended from three months to six, to nine, to well over a year. My first real shock came after *Ring Out an Alibi* had finished. I was scheduled for work in Studio B, the smaller of the two studios in the Broadway chapel. I arrived early to look at the studio and study the floor plan. This was a simple, straightforward discussion involving an interviewer and an interviewee. Two very smart chairs had been set against a clear blue cyclorama and each one had two small microphones facing each chair. The crew arrived and started setting up the cameras, but there was no Geraint. I went upstairs to check what time he was due in on the studio schedule. I went back down to the studio and spoke to the senior cameraman. He did not think Geraint was due in on that day and went to check it out on my behalf.

Five minutes later he returned. No, Geraint was scheduled for something else; this programme was mine to floor manage. I suddenly felt ill. There must be a mistake. I had received no training for this job. Communicating with a gallery two floors above me and being a 'go-between' on the floor between the interviewer and the director up in the box was not my brief. But, apparently it was my brief this time and before I knew it, the studio doors opened and in walked Derek Hart with his guest. To make matters worse the producer of this show was already calling me in my earphones and I had to respond. They must have thought I was a total idiot. I was talking back to him in whispers and sounding unutterably incompetent. The cameramen just stood there and grinned.

"Put Derek on the camera right chair and his guest opposite him on Camera 3," came the instruction from the box. I had to grapple with that one.

Then the secretary called, "David, can you ask Derek what time cues he wants?"

The sound department called me at the same time. "Question and answer from both men please."

"Cameras 1 and 3 – can you show me the captions please?" asked the producer.

There were no captions, they were in a pile on the floor and I should have distributed them to the caption stands for the scene crew to handle. Derek Hart, oh my God! He will think me a total fool. A journalist from the *Tonight* programme, a nightly 40-minute topical magazine programme that came from London and was seen all over the UK, he was from the same stable as Alan Whicker, Fyfe Robertson and Cliff Michelmore. With hesitations in my voice and warbles in my throat, I asked him to take a seat in the right hand chair and put his guest in the opposite one. The cameramen were putting the captions in order and the secretary and the sound department kept asking me the same questions.

"Time cues for Derek please David," requested the secretary.

"Voice levels please," requested the sound department yet again.

I was flummoxed; everyone was speaking at the same time and I could not react fast enough.

"What time cues, Mr Hart please?"

Derek, straightening his tie, looked up at me and said, "One minute, 30 seconds, and a 15-second wind-up will be fine, thank you."

I sought help from the other floor managers that week. They gave me some of the studio procedures, including a hand signals guide for the presenters. They suggested to always arrive early and check captions before rehearsals started and make sure they go to the right camera. The captions might be still photographs, maps, the name of the programme, and introduced by, etc. I was advised to make sure that the presenter and guests had a glass of water each; to check out the presenter's time signals, to look after him or her: in other words, 'look after the talent'. I had to be responsive to the director, make sure the scene crew know what they are doing. Basically, the floor manager was responsible to the producer for the smooth running of the studio floor. I was told to keep discipline, be cheery, always have a smile, be in control and not leave a stone unturned when it came to props and other finite details. They said that in the early 1960s, the divorce rate was low amongst television floor managers – having been pushed from pillar to post by different people, it was a joy to go home and relax with the wife. They would also say (whoever 'they' were) that a good floor manager was the only member of the team who remained calm when everyone around him was pulling their hair out.

After general programming I was back on drama, assisting Islwyn Maelor Evans on a play about a girl who was being terrorised by a young man. It was quite a violent piece, a kind of psychological thriller and the main set in the studio was a dilapidated cinema interior. There was a fair amount of outdoor filming, including a sequence outside Swansea prison in the rain – the rain being produced by the local fire brigade. It was here I remembered my father's words, "They make it all in bits David." Only one camera this time, a film camera shooting shot by shot; a slow tedious process I thought, having been used to the non-stop routine of studios and electronic multi camera set-ups.

It was back to the news studio in Stacey Road. A small, simple studio set-up, but with quick-fire producers who could shoot from the hip and most of the material went live on air. Led by Alan Protheroe, who ran a slick news operation, this was television in the fast lane. Film was still wet from processing as it went through the gate and it was here that my first cousin, Richard Lewis, worked, producing news and documentary material for *Heddiw* and *Wales Today* – a solid foundation for all the fine award-winning television drama he produced in later years in English and in Welsh.

***

At the end of 18 months, my contract with the BBC came to an end. I was heartbroken but fought the termination with a staunch tenacity. There were many colleagues who pleaded my case for wanting me to stay and I dare say my cousin, Richard, would have been speaking out on my behalf, but cut-backs of freelance staff made it an absolute and tragic necessity. I applied through official channels to return to the ranks of the BBC and stated that I would be prepared to do work at any level to find that staff job. It was not to be. I was back on the dole in bedsitter land, and from there I wrote to every television company in the country applying for work.

My work in BBC television had been judged a success. Whereas the theatre had once been my ultimate goal and driving ambition with all its risk and uncertainty, I now saw my past television experience pointing the way forward; 18 months in the BBC studios had been a defining point in my career. Theatre had been my training ground but the magic of television was giving me a real, solid direction. I had felt so comfortable in that television studio and I wanted more. I was also healthier and had a small Post Office savings account. If destiny had any shape or meaning, then it was telling me in the strongest possible voice to go and work in the television or film industry. It was unquestionable, immovable, even. It was fact.

***

Reality kicked in. I was unemployed again. I lay back on my bed with my head propped up against the pillow. The light outside my window was declining and an autumn sunset brought long shadows into my room. The tea in my cup had gone cold and I could not bother to make another. I would take a short nap and maybe go to the cinema later. I stared at the wall, and, yet again, there he was, my running man! He was still there in my wallpaper, the running man, looking mockingly clearer than ever before.

CHAPTER 8

A Seat in the Stalls

THE BLOOD-SPLATTERED LETTER-HEADING read, *The Hammer House of Horror*, and it was one of many responses which came to my bedsit in answer to numerous job-searching enquiries.

'Dear Mr Lloyd, Short of someone accidentally (!) breaking their neck in the near future, or meeting their sad demise in some other unfortunate way, there will be no job vacancies at our studio.'

The letter was both explicit and amusingly tongue-in-cheek and came from Bray in Berkshire. The letters of rejection fell on my mat every morning like snowflakes and made the day ahead depressing and unbearable. The running man on my wallpaper was laughing at my efforts and despite 18 months of employment with the BBC in Cardiff, the experience counted for nothing, it seemed. The woman in the dole office was becoming a real friend, "Any jobs Dave?" I would shake my head, sign the form and go in the following week to collect my money.

Associated Rediffusion was a television company that supplied London with its ITV programmes. They were seeking a studio floor manager and Mr Len Swainston, their senior floor manager, wanted to meet me for an interview. Rediffusion were noted for their programmes on the network, one being, *No Hiding Place*, and amongst many others the pop show, *Ready, Steady, Go!* I went down to their Wembley studio and had a wonderful chat with this man. We talked television and I pressed home my experience with the BBC in Cardiff. The result? No job, but my name would go on file. I was devastated. Maybe I should return to the fruit market, but that would be going back and not forward. I wrote a few short stories for the *Echo* but they were not accepted. Another interview followed in London with a company called Pay Television. The viewer put money into a slot in his living room, chose a film and sat and watched it. They wanted an announcer between films but, surprise, surprise, I was not chosen.

Suddenly, along came pirate radio stations: Radio Caroline, Radio London, Radio 390. I quite fancied the idea of being a DJ and having my own pop radio show; playing pop records on the high seas outside the legal limit, all before BBC Radio One and Two, of course. I wrote letters to them all and they all wrote letters back to me. 'Thank you for taking an interest in our radio station but I am afraid we have received thousands of applications and you were not one of the people chosen etc., etc.' Back to the drawing board mister, and time for a re-think. My dad invited me home but something told me that if I went, I would never get the job I wanted more than anything else in the world, one in television. I applied for a job with a company that made drill-bits and compressors for digging holes in roads. It took a month to realise that I was slowly dying a death through boredom and that nothing in my range of skills had equipped me for caring about drill-bits and compressors or holes in roads.

***

A nasty dose of glandular fever confined me to my bed in that wretched bedsitter for the following three to four weeks. The running man was now having a good laugh at me! The advice from my elders was to consider a job in cinema management. It would take me closer to the visual image and give me a certain quiet dignity, standing on the steps of a picture palace, welcoming the patrons to the second house performance of whatever was showing on the silver screen that week. My

Uncle Alex pronounced the job a doddle, and reminded me that standing dressed in my best bib and tucker, namely dickie-bow, white collar and dark suit and black shoes, every night would give the cinema a certain gravitas, and me, an elevation in life that I sorely needed. I argued my case for a job in television but was told that it was now time to face the real world and put aside all thoughts of messing around in the media. I had given it my best shot but now it was time to live like an 'ordinary person'. All this was quite rich coming from Alex, who had spent a lifetime talking to me about films and the Hollywood stars. The trouble was Alex had spent his life working in the Inland Revenue, counting the days to his retirement. His understanding of cinema management was of a job with all the glitz of a Hollywood movie; the thick carpet underfoot leading you across a dazzling foyer into a wonderfully spacious, plush cinema auditorium where the curtains slowly lifted, the lights dimmed and the screen splashed forth with a cavalcade of magic and make-believe. If I was not convinced, my father was, and I owed my dad more than one or two favours. My letter to one of the largest cinema franchises in the country was posted the following day.

I started work at the Odeon cinema in Balham, south-west London, during the winter months of 1966. The Rank Organisation were paying me £11 a week. I said my goodbyes to Cardiff and that hideous bedsitter with its equally hideous furniture and the running man. I had clung to this city since childhood; it had brought me poverty and riches but now it was time to leave and go out there yet again and find a better future.

***

I was now back in south London, in Balham, which is part of the London Borough of Wandsworth and the London Borough of Lambeth. The people of Balham are warm hearted and those born there included the late John Sullivan, the writer of *Only Fools and Horses*, Jimmy Hill, the sports pundit and former footballer and Dame Margaret Rutherford, the actress. Balham's tube station is featured in Ian McEwan's novel, *Atonement* (2007), which was made into a film some years later. It is noteworthy because it was there that people took cover during a Second World War bombing raid. The station suffered a direct hit, bursting water and gas mains and killing the 64 people sheltering on the station's platform.

The Odeon cinema in Balham High Street in the early 1960s was one of a chain of cinemas all belonging to J. Arthur Rank. Like other Odeon cinemas up and down the country, it was a large, stylish building designed in the maritime-inspired Art Deco style. The multiple front doors opened up to a long stairway which then revealed a spacious foyer, with the booking office and sweetshop on the left, and auditorium straight ahead. In the centre of the foyer, there was a large central staircase to the upper balcony, offices and toilets. The total capacity of this place must have run to well over two thousand seats. The walls of the auditorium were decked in those Art Deco flaps which revealed soft lights. The floors were carpeted throughout and there was a feeling of great luxury about the place. This was a house of exotic style and built at a time when the public could ill afford the trappings of luxuries at home, but would step off the pavements in their thousands and escape to the cinemas where their lives would be transported away from the harsh realities of life in the Twenties, the Thirties and the Forties, to the warmth and comfort of picture palaces with names like The Plaza, the Gaumont, the Regal and the Odeon. However, when I started work in the Balham Odeon in 1966, the fixtures and fittings were beginning to show their age. The golden years of Hollywood were finally over and cinema attendances were in rapid decline because of the spread of television.

Mr Jukes, the manager, fought tooth and claw to uphold the old traditions at the Balham Odeon. He ran the place like a sergeant major. He was short of stature, sported a substantial moustache, hair greased back and dark-rimmed glasses, but made up for his size with the regimental discipline he imposed upon his staff. Any sign of slackness, there would be trouble. He would hire and fire at will and his quick temper made him a figure to be feared and respected. If Mr Jukes walked the carpeted interiors, resplendent in his evening suit, the staff stood to attention and, anyone caught shirking their responsibilities, would be in trouble the following morning. The man's intentions were well meant but more relevant to another age when self-sacrifice and commitment to the cause was part of a structured society. This was the liberated mid 1960s, when young people had adopted their own style and culture, had money in their pockets and questioned the disciplines of a bygone age. I could see immediately there would be anxious days ahead when Mr Jukes's ethics would cross my own, and I hoped I would be man enough to deal with it. I had 18 months of television work under my belt; I was not without experience in the job market and maybe, just maybe, I was not the right candidate for this job. But it was £11 a week in my pocket and I was anxious to prove myself to my family.

"Understand this Mr Lloyd, we are a well-ordered cinema here on a major circuit. Everything that happens within these walls comes under my jurisdiction. The place runs like a well-oiled machine and everyone is expected to pull the ropes and…"

Suddenly there was a knock on his office door.

"Yes," barked Mr Jukes. "Come in." A tall man in dungarees appeared. Everyone talked with a strong Cockney accent or 'Saff' London, if you were a purist. "Ah, Jim, that young bloke you have working with you… is he pulling his weight? By the way, this is Mr Lloyd… he comes to us as a trainee manager."

"Pleased to meet you, Mr Lloyd." I nodded in his direction. A pretty face appeared at the door, with blonde hair tumbling over her shoulders.

"Miss Shepherd, did you get those keys?"

"Yes, Mr Jukes. They were in the ladies' toilet."

"Who left them there, Miss Shepherd?"

"I don't know, Mr Jukes."

"I'm sure you do, Miss Shepherd. We both know who it might have been. We cannot afford to lose keys, Miss Shepherd. Now get out."

"Yes, Mr Jukes."

"Before you go, Miss Shepherd."

"Yes, Mr Jukes."

"Your hair to be pinned up please whilst working here. You know the rules. Do I make myself clear?"

"Yes, Mr Jukes."

"Off you go and... oh, Miss Shepherd, before you go, this is Mr Lloyd, our new trainee manager."

"Nice to meet you, sir," Miss Shepherd smiled timidly in my direction and made her exit.

The phone rang and Mr Jukes barked angrily. "Where is Matty today? She should be answering these calls." He adjusted his tone and mood. "Good morning, Balham Odeon. Yes sir, our doors are open at 2 p.m. with a performance of our main feature at 3 p.m." There is a pause. "Next week we have *The List of Adrian Messenger* – performances at 3, 5, and 7 p.m. Doors open at 2. Thank you." He slammed the phone down and muttered under his breath about the absence of Matty and looked up at Jim, the projectionist.

"Now then, Jim, that new bolt for the second projector is arriving by courier in a few days. Do you need any help to fix it?"

"No thanks, Mr Jukes, I can manage it myself sir, thank you, sir."

"You sure now?"

"Sure as eggs, Mr Jukes."

"Good, off you go."

I wondered if all this dialogue had been for my benefit, but probably not. Staff came and went through his office door with constant regularity, all touching their forelock: cleaners, usherettes, sweetshop attendants, painters, decorators, film and poster distributors, ice cream and confectionery wholesalers, toilet cleaners and plumbers.

Only one lady could play Mr Jukes at his own game and that was Matty Smith, short and slim with the smoothest of features. Pure Cockney of speech, trimmed short hair, half-bitten fingernails, tight skirt, high heels and ultra efficient at paperwork, she managed the shop and the box office, the rota for usherettes and stocks and sales of confectionery. She was Jack and Jill of all trades within those walls and she knew how to give as much 'lip' as she received. Looking back, I have often wondered why she was not assistant manager, but not many women were given that opportunity in those days. She may have lacked boardroom polish but could have learned all that in the fullness of time. Matty had one weakness and it drove Mr Jukes up the wall.

"For God's sake Matty, all you do is chew on blessed eucalyptus mints all day."

That and smoking were her crutches in life. One could smell the eucalyptus as she entered the room. My place was to share the general office with Matty and I could not have wished for anyone better. She was a character, with a little round face and a tiny body, but she knew how to stand her ground against Mr Jukes. She was my breath of fresh mountain air in an environment in which I was feeling more and more out of tune.

The paperwork was horrific. In 1966 there were no electronic spreadsheets. Stock sheets, ledgers and nightly and daily admissions sheets, staff rota and overtime sheets were written by hand and posted to head office. I grappled with the sales of Mars bars, fruit parfaits, Bounties, ice cream tubs and lollipops for days on end. My arithmetic had not improved since my school days and I was constantly asking Matty for help. If learning to add up had been a weakness, I was now the fastest kid on the block in the shop and in the booking ticket office. There was something addictively horrifying in manning the ticket office during a James Bond film, or something equivalent, and seeing a crowd of customers rush like a stampede of bulls towards the pane of glass that divided them from me, eager, excited faces, all wanting a ticket: there was no time for hesitations.

"Three, three and sixes please."

My brain would unscramble the amount, mentally add it up, press the button and out would zoom three, three and sixpenny tickets across the little highly polished brass counter. I hated the experience, and dreaded Saturday morning matinees when besieged by hundreds of grubby-fingered kids all wanting sherbet lemons, crisps, lollipops, black jacks and bubble gum, the latter sticking to the cinema carpets that had all the cleaners up in arms and rapping on Mr Jukes's office door.

My situation was not improved by my salary or my accommodation. In Streatham, my landlady practically owned the entire street. All the houses had been divided into little rooms heated by a one-bar electric fire, and most rooms contained an old age pensioner. Each morning, in all weathers, I would join the line of pensioners walking down the street to our breakfast in number 38. Once again, the breakfast appeared from behind a hatch. One slice of bacon, one sausage and one fried egg, with two pieces of toast. It never changed. The heavy teapots were already on the table, with a small pot of marmalade. This was light industry on a grand scale, and the old people would sit down and eat and then return to their rooms back up the street not uttering a single word to each other. The food, I felt, was not sufficient. The breakfast would have to last me until late into the evening, and so I did my 'Oliver' bit and asked for more. There was none, so my consumption of food was finely judged. Eleven pounds a week and I was as thin as a wafer. I walked to work each day from Streatham to Balham and then from Balham to Streatham late each night. If I could avoid lunch, I would have a blow-out late at night in the nearest burger café.

Sunday was a day for a visit to Nina and Peter's restaurant in Streatham. Not a big Sunday lunch – not that I cared – for my eye was set on a pretty lady with golden blonde hair sitting over on the other side of the café with her parents and sister. One Sunday I followed them to find out where they were going. They went straight down the road to the Silver Blades Ice Rink in Streatham, and whilst mother sat upstairs in the café chatting away, dad, little sister and the blonde lady went skating on the ice. My detective work did not stop there. After several weeks, I pondered my course of action and left a note with the commissionaire at the Silver Blades asking the blonde lady out on a date the following week. She turned up and I took her out for corned beef, egg and chips, and a night at the Streatham Odeon which was a bit of a busman's holiday for me. Annette and her family, who were all delightful people, came into my life at a time when I needed them most. But, inwardly, I knew that something in my life was wrong and that if I was going to make it in cinema management, I would have to buckle down and work harder.

"Mr Lloyd, would you come into my office please?" Mr Jukes was on the warpath. The last performance of that day had started and this was a good time for rows.

"Sit down, Mr Lloyd."

"Yes, sir." Smoothing his moustache with one hand, he looked at me unsmilingly from behind his desk. "I do not get the impression Mr Lloyd that you are entirely happy here. I am looking for commitment and I don't seem to be getting it."

I argued the case with him for two hours that evening, told him that arithmetic was not my strongest point and that those spreadsheets were both confusing and unutterably boring.

"You will sit at my shoulder every day until we crack your little problems with the cash sheets, Mr Lloyd. Do I make myself perfectly clear?"

"Yes, Mr Jukes." I found myself sounding like everyone else on the staff – paying homage to Mr Jukes. He continued:

"Our foyer sales play an important part in our operation here Mr Lloyd. Sales, sales, sales, Mr Lloyd. We have a high turnover in that shop downstairs and head office are more than pleased with our record and whilst I am manager of this cinema, we will..."

The phone rang.

"Yes, madam. Next week we are proud to present *Our Man Flint* with James Coburn. Performances start on Sunday and continue through to Wednesday. Doors open at 2.30 p.m. Performances, 3, 5 and 7p.m. Thank you, bye." He slammed the phone down. "Where is bloody Matty? She should be taking these calls."

I was about to get up and go. "Sit where you are, Mr Lloyd. No one leaves my office without my permission, do I make myself absolutely clear?" I sat down again, my face reflecting the horror of his attitude.

"The usherettes, Mr Lloyd."

"What about the usherettes, Mr Jukes?"

"Erm... " He hesitated.

"Yes, one usherette... in particular. Miss Shepherd, I think it was." He started shuffling the papers on his desk.

"Yes," I replied. "What about Miss Shepherd, Mr Jukes?"

"She has made a complaint, Mr Lloyd."

The door opened and Matty walked in, chewing a eucalyptus sweet.

"GET OUT... AND THROW AWAY THAT BLOODY SWEET," yelled Mr Jukes. She disappeared as quickly as she had appeared.

"Yes, now where were we?" Mr Jukes regained his composure.

"Miss Shepherd and her complaint, Mr Jukes."

"Ah yes... she said you... touched her, Mr Lloyd. Made a pass at her. Can this be true?" I froze in horror and stared at him. I felt for a moment that I was on stage in a gripping three-act play, and then reality kicked in.

There was a knock at the door. "COME," yelled Jukes. It was Mrs Jukes bringing her husband a late-night sandwich and a nice hot cup of tea from the flask she carried in her tea-cloth covered basket, looking much like Little Red Riding Hood. It was all quite bizarre.

"Hello my dear, come in. Mr Lloyd was just leaving. We will talk in the morning, Mr Lloyd. Thank you. You go now. I will lock up tonight." I left his office feeling numb. What he had said could not have been further from the truth.

I could not afford to eat that night. I walked home a hungry man. As I entered the house, I could hear the old pensioners snoring in their beds. I entered my room without putting the light on, lay on the bed and fell into a troubled sleep.

CHAPTER 9

Raspberry Ripples and Riots

SOMEHOW I FELT that my previous BBC job had been of greater importance than the one I was holding in the cinema. The cinema was a retrograde step in my opinion and did not sit comfortably in my overall plans for working in television despite what the family in Cardiff and Aberystwyth were saying. Sooner or later I would have to confide in Jukes and be honest and upfront.

I stood my ground solidly in the Miss Shepherd affair and dared Jukes to call the woman into the office. He loved confrontation but this was one shouting match he was not going to pursue. I was not altogether sure whether the story had been invented. Matty suggested I took a deep breath and let things drop. She was, as always, right. From then on, Jukes had me shadowing him everywhere. We stood on the steps each evening, me in my Dunn and Co. dark green tweed jacket with a white shirt and black dickie bow. My meagre wage would not allow me a trip to Moss Bros. We chatted to patrons and gave people the impression that this cinema had gravitas.

Sunday evenings was the time Mr Jukes exercised his prerogative and started the evening's performance by pressing a button on the back wall of the auditorium which rang two floors upstairs in the projection box. Every other day of the week, the projectionist started the performance by watching the time. On Sunday, owing to increased audiences with the opening of cinemas on the Sabbath, Mr Jukes would keep a steady eye on admissions and put the start of performance under his own control.

"Mr Lloyd, you can ring the bell tonight, I will be doing the paperwork in the office."

"Certainly Mr Jukes, it will be a pleasure."

As I entered the auditorium, the usherettes stood to attention. Miss Shepherd smiled. "Quite a lot in tonight, Mr Lloyd," the other girls nodding and agreeing with her. I had an overwhelming desire to pat her on the bum and announce to the waiting customers that there would be no performance tonight as Miss Shepherd and I would be eloping on the next train to Gretna Green. I thought the better of it but I was at least making light of my situation. I pressed the button, the houselights dimmed, the curtains opened and the evening's performance started. I could feel the power surging through my veins!

During a heated discussion one day, I happened to tell Mr Jukes that audiences did not bother me and that I had a background in live theatre. He enquired further and called me closer to his desk.

"There is one job I would like you to do, Mr Lloyd, that I would prefer not to do myself on this occasion."

Fire drill was important and what was about to happen has made me laugh uproariously to this day. The plan was to walk out on stage in the middle of a film and announce to the audience that they should leave the cinema via the nearest exit, at which point the usherettes would position themselves at exit doors and shout, "This way. This way." The film would stop and the house lights would come on. At least, that was the plan. Sunday afternoon seemed an appropriate time to conduct the exercise as there were a fewer number of paying patrons present. The grand moment arrived and Jukes stood with me in the wings.

"You sure you still want to do this?" he asked.

The sound from the film boomed out of three enormous speakers and Rock Hudson and Doris Day were bigger than

I had ever seen them before. The moment came and I was given the signal by Jukes. I walked out on stage and faced the audience, microphone in hand.

"Good afternoon ladies and gentlemen..."

I had Doris Day around my armpits one moment and then Rock Hudson emblazoned across my forehead the next.

"This is an emergency ladies and gentlemen. Would you please leave by the nearest exit in an orderly fashion."

On the word 'emergency' the usherettes from all corners of the auditorium pushed open the exit doors and screamed like a bunch of hyenas.

"THIS WAY, THIS WAY, THIS WAY."

In the meantime the angry audience, made up largely of south London youths started pelting me with every object they could lay their hands on. Flying out of the darkness came ice-cream tubs, raspberry ripples, plimsolls and fruit parfaits. The lights came on and I faced my assailants, a gathering of annoyed youths bent on ruining my Sunday afternoon.

"OUT," I shouted, pointing to the doors. There was a distinct smell of vanilla on my suit and my trousers had taken on the complexion of a cherry trifle. Mr Jukes promised to pay for the cleaning out of the petty cash tin and the afternoon was deemed a success.

The second incident, involving the youth of Balham, came one day when Mr Jukes and Matty were locked in verbal combat over the wretched paperwork. I was sitting taking it all in. There was a sudden knock at the door.

"Come," growled Jukes. An usherette stepped in.

"Please Mr Jukes, there is trouble down in the stalls... some boys... black and white..."

Matty was about to dash out and sort out the problem herself.

"SIT DOWN, MATTY."

He adjusted his tone, continued to look down at the spreadsheets on his desk and muttered, "Go and sort it out please Mr Lloyd will you?" I joked back and said something about my last will and testament and left his office.

The auditorium that afternoon had black people sitting down one side and white kids on the other. There had been a scuffle and knives had been drawn. I took a deep breath and walked the aisle. There was some rubbish on the carpet and I asked a youth to pick it up and take it home. He did as instructed and sat back in his seat. I walked the aisles two or three times to imply I was keeping an eye on them and not a kid moved – all eyes glued to the screen. Obviously my presence had been enough to stem the problem. Jukes, Matty and I observed the troublemakers leaving the cinema that afternoon; Jukes instructed Matty to check between the rows of seats.

**

My final involvement with the rough and tough came late one evening when Jukes was on holiday. A retired freelance manager with a couldn't-care-less attitude had been brought in to supervise. Matty did all the paperwork, all he did was to add his signature. He was tossing the day's takings around in a muslin bag and pulling out the keys for the safe-deposit box down in the foyer. The safe was directly under a large mirror which was a mad place to put it by today's security standards.

"This cinema business is a bloody mad business, don't you think Mr Lloyd? These places won't last I can guarantee you that. They are like old dinosaurs and will end up under the hammer, you mark my words. I would get out if I were you."

This man was harmless enough and we laughed. Downstairs in the foyer, we opened up the safe revealing the thickness of the steel interior. Still in his playful mood, he said, "How would you like this little lot in your wage packet each month?"

I smiled and looked up and, reflected in the mirror, were five men in their early twenties. One was combing his thick, greasy hair, the other holding a knife.

"OK, you men, hand over the bag otherwise there will be trouble."

I froze to the spot. Five dangerously armed men against us were impossible odds. The old man rose from his knees and looked straight at them. Suddenly he started to swing the cash bag around again and use it like a weapon.

"You f*** off you filthy scum, get out of this cinema. Who do you think you're f******g dealing with? Get out of here before I call the police."

The men stepped back and made a beeline for the door, with the old man still shouting abuse at them. I started to breathe again but I was shaken to the core.

"They were just pushing their luck, Mr Lloyd. Just kids." Our stand-in manager had saved the day but his devil-may-care-attitude may have seen them off and yet, at the same time, encouraged them.

When Jukes returned I discovered he had a nose for smelling out the trouble that had taken place in his absence. With members of staff who would blow the whistle on others, he soon had all the facts before him on the table. He called Matty and me into his office and the interrogation began. On a second day, he called the freelance manager in and myself. The afternoon developed a nastiness which almost had the deputising manager and myself reaching for each other's throats. Jukes seemed to enjoy it, for the whistle-blowing came from both sides of the ring.

"You bloody nasty little Welshman," said the deputising manager.

"That's rich coming from you... you English bastard," I replied.

"Gentlemen, gentlemen," Jukes interrupted and the afternoon fizzled away like so many other confrontations in Mr Jukes's office. Looking back, I was even more convinced he enjoyed them.

I am not particularly proud of that moment in my life, although I had learned to defend my corner and not take matters too seriously. The incident, however, did prompt me to inform Jukes that I was not a happy man and that I would be making every effort to find alternative employment in the near future. The decision prompted senior executives in the Rank organisation to call me up to head office to undergo a series of psychological tests. The questions alternated between whether I could see myself as a captain of a rugby team to whether I could ever envisage myself winning a Morris dancing championship. I saw little point in the exercise and developed a dismissive attitude towards such foolish questions. I also made it abundantly clear that my wages were poor and that I could barely keep body and soul together in London.

The executives then sent me on a management course around several cinemas that never seemed to end. My only recollection of a trip to Kilburn was from a fellow trainee manager who informed me that he had managed to make love to his girlfriend in a bubble car. I laughed out loud and admired him for setting the record. After Kilburn it was down to a cinema in King's Cross. This place was like a lighthouse, built on the corner of a busy London street. The young manager had his leg in plaster and a wonderful sense of humour.

"I'll sit here David and do all the paperwork if you do the walking around the cinema and keep an eye on the front of house."

It was an arrangement that suited me just fine. The London underground lines ran directly under this place which had the audience vibrating in their seats every ten minutes, every five during rush hour. The manager made me laugh. He was so relaxed and nonchalant, and I was genuinely sorry when my time in King's Cross came to an end. I signed his plaster cast with fondest thanks for the beer at lunchtime and that tonic of daily laughter. Then it was on to the Rochester Odeon for a Sunday afternoon pop concert from the Spencer Davis group and The Who. This was before the days of barricades at such events. I was instructed to stand with five other lads, equally spaced with our backs to the stage, protecting the pop groups from the sea of mad women that were threatening to bulldoze their way over the footlights and cause carnage, mayhem and mischief to any young man who sang and played a guitar. It was like facing a pack of hungry wolves. Knickers and bras were taken off and thrown in the air and the swell moved towards us like a huge storm at sea. This was my first experience of a riot.

The music blasted out from enormous amplifiers and the young girls rushed the stage with lust in their eyes. This was a gladiatorial spectacle on a grand scale. We fought them off with fury, swelling our chests out and pretending to be seasoned bouncers. They were gasping to get closer and the music inflamed their feelings even more. We suffered a few cuts and bruises but, other than that, I and the other lads survived the riot and the pop groups survived to play another day.

It was then back to the Balham Odeon and back to Jukes and Matty. I would talk at length with her and gaze out of the window at the evening sky over the chimney pots and rooftops of Balham. We enjoyed laughing at most things. She was good company in a place where there was not much cheerfulness. Her grasp of the paperwork was so much better than mine. She smoked constantly and chewed those sweets until the whole room was full of the smell of eucalyptus.

Monday morning and time for a meeting with Mr Jukes.

"Are you happier now Mr Lloyd?"

"No, sir. I don't really believe this is the career for me. I have made a mistake and I will be the first to admit it. I have appreciated everything you have done for me but I do not think cinema management is the career for me." Blimey, I thought. I am signing my own death warrant here.

He took a cigarette out of a packet and offered me one. We sat and smoked silently. Matty entered.

"Sit down, Matty. Nothing here is secret from you."

She sat silently and looked across at me and half smiled. Jukes had changed. He was more mellow and less aggressive.

Had anyone from head office talked to him I wondered. There was another long pause.

"What do you really want to do Mr Lloyd? What do you feel your real vocation to be?"

I answered almost immediately.

"Broadcasting, Mr Jukes. I once worked in television and I would give all I have, not that I have much mind you, to return there. I am grateful for everything you have shown me. None of it has been a waste of time but my chief interest is what is on that screen... the film... and how it is made. The sales of ice cream and bubble gums hold no interest for me whatsoever. I'm sorry."

"Stop biting your nails Matty... please," Jukes commanded.

He looked across at me. There was another pause.

"I have a friend who works for ABC Television, Mr Lloyd. I will have a word with him for you."

He winked across at me.

I nearly fell off my seat in dumbstruck surprise. Mr Jukes, despite the cage of iron that surrounded him, had shown me a gesture of kindness. It was quite extraordinary after all this time. I thanked him sincerely. He stubbed out his cigarette in the ashtray and rose from his desk.

"Get off to work both of you. We have a cinema to run."

***

I woke the following morning and picked up a letter that had been posted to me from somewhere in Cardiff. It was typewritten and had been sent to my old Cardiff flat, and some kind-hearted soul had forwarded it. Doubtless another rejection; I had files full of them. I tucked it away in my inside jacket pocket. It was not until some hours later in the cinema that I suddenly remembered the letter and over a cup of coffee I decided to rip it open, read the sad news and throw it in the bin.

There were two letters – one from Jean, a friend living in the flat above mine in Cardiff, and another. I read Jean's letter first.

Dear David.
  The enclosed letter came to the house and must have been read by Mrs Foster 'cause the envelope had been ripped open and its contents read by her. Anyway, it had fallen under the telephone table and is probably of no interest to you now as you are comfortably settled in a new job. I am however, sending it on to you, although Mrs Foster does not think it will be of any interest.
  Hope you are happy and keeping well and enjoying your new job.
  Love,
  Jean xx

I then read the enclosed which was headed Anglia Television Ltd.

Dear Mr Lloyd
  We are seeking a freelance floor manager for the summer period to work in one of our smaller studios in Norwich. Mr Len Swainston of Associated Rediffusion in Wembley has passed on your name to us as being a suitable candidate.
  Please would you call the Personnel Department at the above number to arrange an interview as quickly as possible.
  Yours sincerely
  Frank O'Shea

My hands were shaking and I spilt my coffee. Matty asked me if everything was all right. I was speechless. Anglia television in Norwich wanted to interview me and that lovely man in Associated Rediffusion had kept my name on the top of his file. My heart was pounding faster than normal and I was in a whirlwind of a panic. I could not believe my luck.

"What is it David, do tell," asked Matty. I looked up at her. I was afraid to let go of the letter.

"Anglia Television want me to attend an interview in Norwich; I can't believe it," I said.

I handed Matty the letter. There were tears in my eyes and then something occurred to me. When had that letter been sent to Cardiff? What was the date on it? After some rapid calculation, I reckoned that there had been a four-day delay between the letter leaving Anglia via Cardiff and arriving at my Tooting address. Soon there would be a fifth day and Anglia Television would give up the chase and seek someone else.

"Matty, I need to ring them now. Time is of the essence. I could be too late already." I reached for the phone.

"Don't ring from here," Matty screeched. "Jukes is in his office and if he comes in, that might mean the end of everything. You go out. There's a phone box down the High Street. Go, quick, quick! I will cover for you."

"Thanks Matty, I love you."

"Go quick you mad Welshman. Jukes will be in here before you've gone."

I ran as fast as my legs could take me, down the stairs to the foyer, out of the front door and zoomed down to the nearest High Street telephone box.

I found a vacant phone box and scrambled in, papers flying everywhere. Attempting to sound cool and relaxed I made connection with Anglia Television. Trying to control my breathing, I asked the switchboard for Personnel. A lady answered. The conversation was brief but I was not too late in my response. They were, however, beginning to wonder if their letter had fallen on deaf ears. Had it not been for Jean in Cardiff, there is no saying what would have happened to my life. I have often pondered the perilous twists and turns.

"When can you get here for an interview, Mr Lloyd?" I sensed urgency in her voice.

"Soon," I said in my excitement, "I mean... how about tomorrow?"

"That would be fine. If you are coming up from London, you will need to get to the Liverpool Street station; the trains to Norwich are fairly frequent. Shall we say 2.30 tomorrow afternoon here at the television centre which is right next door to the post office. You can't miss us. Just walk straight up towards the town centre."

I thanked her profusely, put the phone down and rang Annette, my girlfriend, at work. I then rang home to Aberystwyth. My Dad and Mum drew their own conclusions at my news but wished me the very best of luck. I kept pinching myself to prove the whole thing was real. After so much disappointment, after so many rejections, at last a chance to prove myself of worth to an ITV company. I walked slowly back to the Odeon. The next hurdle was Jukes. Would he give me the day off tomorrow? Please, please let him give me the day off tomorrow.

"May I take tomorrow off please, Mr Jukes?" He looked across at me with a blank expression.

"Any particular reason, Mr Lloyd?"

"I have an interview with Anglia Television in Norwich tomorrow afternoon, sir."

No mention was made of his friend with ABC Television in London.

"Are you sure this is what you want Mr Lloyd; moving from a reasonably safe and secure job to something which is... temporary, shall we say?"

"I want it more than anything else, Mr Jukes. Television is definitely my future."

Looking through the train window on my way up to Norwich the following day, I thought through those brave words to Jukes. If I didn't get the job with Anglia, he would be sitting there with that wry smile on his face, smoothing his moustache, looking across the room at me and saying, "I did warn you Mr Lloyd."

I arrived in Norwich with plenty of time. Time for some lunch and to buy a copy of *TV Times* to see what kind of programmes Anglia Television made. That knowledge could be useful for the interview. The train fare had taken most of my money. I had enough cash to buy a bread roll stuffed with corned beef to eat by the river and watch some local fishermen. I was not nervous, my BBC experience was well forward in my mind and I would talk about that, if asked. I would use my cheerful personality and assure them of three dedicated months of work.

The interview with Mr Frank O'Shea was more of a chat than a real interview. It was not dissimilar to the Associated Rediffusion interview, friendly and accommodating. *Weaver's Green*, the first so-called 'soap' of its kind, although the word 'soap' was not in common use then, was taking up most of Anglia's resources. They were, therefore, looking for a floor manager to work in their smaller studio which did news, current affairs, farming and children's programmes. He asked me what I was currently doing. I told him I was doing some work for the Rank Organisation and that giving notice would not be a problem. He was also interested in what I had been doing with the BBC in Cardiff and in the theatre.

"Good, that's it David, well done, the job is yours. We will send you a letter of temporary engagement over the next few days. Oh, by the way, your salary will be £1,766 per annum. Expenses will be paid when necessary. Happy with that?"

I nodded my head and shook his hand warmly. I was euphoric.

"Linda in that office over there will reimburse you your expenses for coming up today. Must rush, see you soon. Call us with your starting date."

I could not stop thanking him.

From here on in, dear reader, you will have to understand that I left the building in a trance-like condition. The sounds of the world outside were muffled and my eyes were filled with tears of gladness and relief. On my desk I still have that letter of confirmation from Anglia Television asking me to sign the carbon copy of their letter of acceptance and to return it to them. It is dated the 20 June 1966. I was 26 years of age; I had been away from home for six strenuous years. I rang my parents and told them the good news and my Dad asked me how much they were paying me. When I told him there was a long pause on the other end of the telephone. He turned to my Mum and whispered, "Good God, the boy is getting more than me."

Jukes was pleased in his own way; he was not a man to show his feelings but, underneath, I think he understood. Matty was delighted and gave me a big hug. When the time of my departure came they both saw me to the top of the steps. It was Matty's turn to cry.

"You really are a crazy Welshman, David Lloyd."

I never saw either of them again and have often wondered what became of them. Maybe one day, in my dotage, I shall make a trip to Balham to find out the answers. On the other hand, it may be advisable to just cherish the memories.

I stayed with Independent Television for the next 31 years.

CHAPTER 10

The Knight in Shining Armour

I WENT HUNGRY, for the last time, in July 1966. Having said farewell to Balham, SW12, Anglia Television paid me at the end of each month which meant I had to eke out a living in Norwich between my starting date on the fourth and payday on the 31st. Over the years, I had developed a system to ward off the hunger pangs and that was to get to bed early and sleep away the complaining stomach. It made breakfast all the more enjoyable. Annette would often say that I would arrive on the Norwich train at a London station, looking as undernourished as a prisoner of war, with my striped pyjamas hanging out of my suitcase. Gradually, as the end of the month grew closer, desperation took hold and my father sent me a cheque for £20. I had so much to thank him for. The cheque arrived in the post on a Saturday morning when the banks were closed and the weekend was spent eating bread and jam. On the Monday, after a visit to the bank, I stuffed down a glorious breakfast in the studio canteen. At the end of that week I was paid my first salary cheque and I felt like a millionaire. Not even the BBC freelance salary in Cardiff could match it. I felt wealthy, I felt wonderful, I could go anywhere, do anything, Having been knocked back so many times I could, at last, put hand on heart and, in the six long years since leaving home in Aberystwyth, say that I had truly made it.

***

The Television Act of 1954 paved the way for the introduction of independent television in the UK. From 1955 onwards, independent television companies were springing up all over the country, breaking up what had been a BBC monopoly in the UK. The whole system would be governed by an overlord, namely the ITA (Independent Television Authority), and they would ensure that these regional companies did not follow the American route and combine advertisements with programmes. A sharp distinction was drawn up between the two and one was not allowed to influence the other. American presenters saying, '... and this programme is brought to you by Tide Soap powder', or whatever the product happened to be, was definitely not allowed; the independent television companies were bound by regulation, and franchises could be lost if that rule was broken. There would be a limit set on the amount of advertising in an hour of programming and guidelines were drawn up to ensure responsible broadcasting.

Roy Thomson, the chairman of Scottish Television described the owning of any ITV franchise as 'a licence to print money'. How right he was. In 1965, the ban on advertising cigarettes on ITV resulted in an £8 million loss of revenue. All the revenue in any ITV company came from advertising, with no part of it coming (as many people believed) from their television licence – that was strictly for the BBC.

Lew Grade, a supreme impresario with strong interests in commercial television in London and the Midlands, tried to keep down the cost of Roger Moore in *The Saint* by telling him episodes would last half an hour and not an hour. However, forever mindful of the impact of ITV, particularly during the making of *Jesus of Nazareth*, Lord Grade asked, "Why are there only twelve apostles?"

Born in the Ukraine and of Jewish descent, Sir Lew Grade, who later became Lord Grade, was brought up in London's East End; his knowledge of what made good film and television was unsurpassed. He was one of those unforgettable characters in those early days of ITV that I would love to have met. Not only did he understand what the audiences wanted, but he invested money in programmes that he knew would make a handsome profit. Whilst discussing the ground-breaking *Jesus of Nazareth*, it was decided that the part of Jesus should be played by a fresh, unknown face. Jokingly, Francis Essex, the ATV production controller suggested that maybe Lord Grade himself might like to play the part. Lord Grade, appearing through a great cloud of Havana cigar smoke replied, "If you cast me you will have to change the ending!" Robert Powell played the role.

Lord Grade was often more right than he was wrong but, when disasters occurred, there always remained an utterance from the great man that, in television and film, parlance would be inscribed in stone. Clive Cussler's book *Raise the Titanic* had been made into a film with terrifying spiralling costs and, to make matters worse, the film bombed at the box office to which Lord Grade was heard to say, "It would have been cheaper to have lowered the Atlantic."

When I watched ITV with my cousins in 1957/8 in Cardiff, I thought it was absolutely stupendous. The local and national programmes were so different – it all made the BBC look rather starchy. On a purely local level again, TWW (Television Wales and the West) had its local celebrities, people like Alan Taylor, Christine Godwin, John Mead, Bruce Lewis and Marian Davies. Together with 22-year-old Maureen Staffer, these people became household names in south Wales and the West Country. Wyn Roberts, later a Welsh MP, was the controller of programmes. One programme that became one of TWW's greatest hits was *Land of Song* with Ivor Emmanuel, Marion Davies and Sian Hopkins. Such was its popularity that it was transmitted live on a Sunday evening to the whole country. The songs were often sung against a rural studio back-drop, with gates and fences and farmyards full of live chickens and geese and other such creatures, and singers would sing with 'hwyl' and gusto, stepping through the animal muck on the studio floor.

TWW's chief announcer, John Mead, claimed that if people

spotted him up in the south Wales valleys, they practically tore the shirt off his back. When not presenting programmes, Alan Taylor, A TWW presenter, was constantly opening shops, church bazaars and country carnivals.

It is said that the BBC, in order to keep its audience, countered the opening night of ITV by killing off Grace Archer in *The Archers* but, no matter how many words were written and spoken against the fledgling channel, it became worthy opposition to the BBC with iconic programmes like *Coronation Street*, *Armchair Theatre*, *The Saint*, *Emergency Ward 10*, *The Avengers*, *The Prisoner*, *Double Your Money* and *Sunday Night at the London Palladium*. ITV also brought in the best of the American market, namely *Rawhide*, *I Love Lucy*, *The Dick Van Dyke Show*, *Sunset Strip*, *Burke's Law* and *Dragnet*. The public loved it all and even sang the jingles from their favourite commercials. The profits were breathtaking and in Wales in 1958 as elsewhere, there was no shortage of board members and investors for TWW: Lord Derby, Jack Hilton, *News of the World*, Imperial Tobacco, *The Daily Post*, Sir Harry Llewelyn, Huw T. Edwards, Sir Ifan ap Owen Edwards and Viscount Cilcennin.

Whether we liked it or not, and most of us liked it, ITV had arrived and was here to stay.

***

When I reported for work on my first day at Anglia Television in 1966, the company had already been running since 1959 – it was a franchise with strong rural links brought together by Lord Townshend, a leading Norfolk farmer. The studio had been an old agricultural hall which in the past had been used for cattle shows and banquets. The studios were housed within a new structure which was purpose-built inside the original building. It was very impressive but the one thing that remains in the minds of older people today about Anglia Television is the company logo – a distinctive symbol called the 'Anglia

Knight'. It was a silver knight in shining armour sitting on his horse holding a standard that bore the name, Anglia. The whole piece revolved on a sort of cake stand in glorious black and white, and the image became synonymous with so many distinctive programmes on the ITV Network. Their region was a large one covering the east of England primarily, but overlapping with central, northern and southern England too. God is no respecter of television boundaries and signals and strong overlap areas occurred almost everywhere – it even happens today. Anglia's role was to provide a strong regional service with its own local news and current affairs, plus other programmes with strong regional content. It encouraged local talent, but also felt it had an important role to play in supplying programmes, especially drama, to national audiences.

I was initially slow but unruffled. I had been away from the industry for some time, the mental speed and the physical agility to work the floor of a live news/magazine programme took a bit of getting used to. The programme directors were razor sharp and the technical crews, although friendly enough, were ultra efficient; they had worked the programme so many times before. David Frost had worked on *About Anglia* in 1960, so I had missed him by six years. My pleasure was to work with many fine broadcasters in that studio. John McGregor and Bob Wellings were such professional people in front of the camera on that particular programme. So clean-cut, such clear, friendly voices and attractive men to look at on any television set. They both dressed and spoke impeccably.

My mind raced through the tasks. Standards had to be set: do not leave a stone unturned, remember the hard lessons of the theatre and of the BBC.

"Check each presenter is comfortable. Come on, move, move, move! Check that their stories tally with yours and yours with the gallery upstairs. Close and lock the studio doors. Check the caption stands, check your talk-back. The red light is on, warning others outside that we are approaching live transmission, pass on any notes of instruction to the two presenters from the director and production assistant upstairs. Check the floor is clear of obstacles for cameras to move quickly and silently without hazard. Check all the crew are present. Give Wardrobe permission to brush presenters' jacket lapels; Make-up assistant to comb hair and to dab off beads of perspiration from foreheads. Ask both presenters to give a sound check by speaking a few lines from their script..."

They do so whilst cutting and writing ad lib remarks. They both knew how to write effectively under pressure and handle the panics of a live news and magazine programme; they could edit the script on the spot and could write for the speaking voice, and that was a very special gift believe you me.

"Don't forget to mark the floor where the weatherman should stand so he does not go out of light. Drop story six Bob, and John can you re-insert paragraph two in story nine please?"

"Will do," he shouts back.

"One minute to transmission," calls the PA through my cans.

In those days there was no autocue – the device that placed the rolling words right in front of the camera lens and enabled the newsreader to look at you, the viewer, and read at the same time. These men could use the camera lens and the paper script all at the same time, effortlessly. They would soon be talking to thousands of viewers, or maybe just one. It was one person or a family in a living room, that's all. We tried not to think of the thousands. We were on air.

The presenters could not hear the director talking to them. They relied entirely on the floor manager. Messages were delivered verbally when we were on a film insert or were given in a series of hand signals from under the camera lens.

"Tell Michael Hunt that he will have two and half minutes for the weather, David."

I pass the message on. He nods and gives a thumbs up. During interviews, I crouched on the floor putting myself in the eye-line of Bob Wellings who was conducting the interview, and gave him hand signals for time left to the end of the interview.

"Two minutes of programme time left. Check the caption stands have the right closing captions. Check that John has the right story to read after Bob has finished his interview. Always check, everything. Don't leave anything to chance. Remember those lessons in the BBC, boy. One minute, 30 seconds, 15 seconds, 10, 9, 8, 7, 6, 5, 4, 3, 2, 1, CUT-THROAT!, CUT-THROAT!, CUT-THROAT! Rise quickly, FAST, FAST, FAST before the camera pedestal knocks you off your knees, and watch the cable on your cans otherwise you will strangle yourself or lose your cans and you will be without talk-back and the show will be free-wheeling and collapsing around you, and the director and the PA will be having a haemorrhage and screaming their heads off upstairs."

My brain races.

"MOVE FAST, MOVE FAST, MOVE FAST! Quick, Quick, Quick... and make a point, after the show, of thanking the presenters, the interviewees and the studio crew before you leave the studio. The studio is yours man, you are in charge, sort it out... MOVE, MOVE, MOVE!"

I was earning my money and loving every minute of it.

**

From that studio in Anglia House came all the bread and butter programmes and, like TWW in south Wales, this station too had its personalities. People like the wonderfully moustached Michael Hunt who always did a perfect job standing at a very basic weather map – basic by today's hi-tech standards – and also Dick Joice, the smoothest of presenters with whom I worked on *Police Call*.

The larger studio was devoted to *Weavers Green*, supposedly television's first rural soap, launched in the time I was there in 1966. Not unlike *Emmerdale* today, it was all about a rural community based in East Anglia. Unfortunately, the transmission times or, slots, as we called them, were not the best times for the viewers. The ITV Network dropped *Weavers Green* after 49 episodes.

***

Local beauty contests were highly popular on television in the 1960s. Older viewers will recall Eric Morley who was the big name behind Mecca. He popularised bingo, catering, gambling, ice skating and bowling alleys, but is remembered best of all for the Miss World beauty competitions. Anglia Television, mindful of its duty to the most beautiful women of the region, would hold a beauty contest in Great Yarmouth. *Glamour 66* was an important outside broadcast (OB).

Any outsider witnessing the first 'stagger-through' of a major OB would be surprised to find themselves amongst absolute chaos. The director is talking his way through the show in the van outside, telling cameras what kind of shots he is looking for, lights are being adjusted, ladders are being moved, people are running around, painters and designers are putting the finishing touches to the set and sound department are taking sound levels from girls and judges alike. There is noise, bedlam and confusion everywhere. Slowly and methodically the show begins to take shape, but you would never believe it from observation. There are band calls, where the sound department take a level-check from every instrument, the director gives notes to everyone, meal times are observed and there are further rehearsals in the afternoon. By 6 p.m. in the evening, nerves are beginning to jangle. The dress run is not without its attendant problems but soon it is time to allow the audience to enter.

During transmission I had one of the finest jobs in this production: looking after the girls behind the set, relaxing them, making them smile and cueing them onto the walkway to take their place on the red carpet to display their trim figures in bathing costumes and evening dresses and to acknowledge the thunderous applause and fanfares that were to follow. *Glamour 66* was considered by all to be a great success for Anglia Television and its loyal viewers. I was, indeed, the luckiest of men in the industry.

***

I worked on one other outside broadcast for Anglia Television, a totally different experience to *Glamour 66*. What made *Tavern Talk* so exciting was not only the fact that it was held in a pub with all the clientele coming and going, but the fact that the presenters were Bob Wellings, again, and the weathered face of broadcaster, traveller and writer, René Cutforth. Basically, it was a chat show with various personalities from the village pub – anyone with a good story to tell. The musical interludes were provided by various Norfolk folk groups.

Anglia Television held its franchise for the east of England for many years to come; it was, as originally intended by Lord Townshend, a prolific supplier of programmes to the ITV Network whilst maintaining strong links with the local community. John Jacobs, brother to David Jacobs, the television and radio personality, was a prolific drama producer there for many years. Keith Hatfield, a journalist at the Anglia TV newsroom went on to work for Independent Television News (ITN) in London and Bob Wellings became a popular presenter on the BBC's *Nationwide* programme.

I suppose the two most popular network programmes from the Anglia stable that still remain fresh in people's minds are *Tales of the Unexpected* created by Roald Dahl and *Survival*, a successful nature and wildlife series created by Aubrey Buxton, later Baron Buxton of Alsa. The series ran from 1961 and won over 250 awards worldwide. For me, *Tales of the Unexpected* will be remembered for Ron Grainer's abstract but chilling opening music and the silhouette of that shapely girl dancing. The stories were sinister, sometimes comic, and the programmes ran from 1979 to 1988 giving gainful employment to many actors including Sir John Gielgud, Dame Anna Neagle, Timothy West, Ian Holm and many others. Roald Dahl introduced each programme from his armchair and the stories were compulsive viewing.

I was now supremely confident that I could do the job well – I had experience with the BBC in Cardiff and Anglia Television in Norwich. It was time now to ply my trade and find a willing employer to offer me work. Money was no longer the problem that it had been, Anglia had seen to that. I had made a note of a few vacancies for studio floor managers some weeks prior to leaving Norwich. The funny thing was I did not feel worried as on previous occasions. Destiny, I inwardly felt, had mapped out a path for me. How silly is that? I collected my last pay cheque plus expenses, said goodbye to Anglia Television, thanked them and, clutching my suitcase, walked down the hill to the railway station. What next I thought to myself, as a cold tingle of anticipation shot down my spine.

CHAPTER 11

The Place where the Typhoid Comes From

WITH NO IMMEDIATE prospect of a job, Annette, my new girlfriend from Orpington, and I had decided to visit Aberystwyth for a week. It was an opportunity for her to meet my folks and a chance for me to catch my breath after three hectic summer months at Anglia Television. A break by the sea and a chance to show her around my home town was as good as any rest.

One warm evening, as the late summer sun cast a shaft of brightness through the window and across the floor to our tea-table, the phone rang. It was James Buchan, controller of programmes for Grampian Television in Aberdeen. He was in London and wanted to meet me for an informal interview. Looking back, my parents at this stage were unintentionally very comical. The table was cleared and a road atlas was produced to find out where Aberdeen was.

"Good Lord," said my father. "According to this atlas, Aberdeen is up in the north of Scotland!"

The sentence was delivered as if he was expecting the place to be moved at any time, all depending on your choice of atlas. "Ah," he then added, remembering something he'd once read in the newspaper. "That's the place where the typhoid comes from."

My mother looked at him with astonishment. "Well,

the same could be said of Aberystwyth in 1947." We all laughed.

The interview was very informal with no boardroom setting: it was just the controller and myself. His gentle presence impressed me but he did strike me as being more like a bank manager than a television man. Dressed in a warm tweed suit, he looked distinguished, with a fullish figure, a weathered but kindly face, glasses, thin, swept back hair, a small grey beard and a soft Scottish lilt to his voice. I could see him living a quiet life with his faithful dog near tumbling mountain streams and slopes adorned with purple heather. He told me little of the programmes for which he was responsible, although he did tell me that Grampian Television offered a strong regional service to its viewers and covered the north and north-east of Scotland taking in towns like Dundee, Inverness, Aberdeen and also the Scottish Highlands.

Grampian Television, originally called North of Scotland Television Ltd had won its franchise against stiff competition; seven other interested parties had made bids. The company was unhappy with the name until some bright person suggested, 'Scottish and Highlands Independent Television', which would have been acceptable had not some other bright person come along and reminded everyone that the initials were hardly appropriate. Grampian Television was chosen instead and the on-screen logo proudly carried the St Andrew's emblem.

The fledgling station went on air in September 1961, with Sir Alexander King as chairman. Sir Ivone Kirkpatrick, chairman of the Independent Television Authority, in an opening broadcast, said that he hoped viewers would come to regard Grampian Television as an essential part of everyday life. Unfortunately, the viewers had other ideas and the company, for many reasons, not unlike the stricken TWW (Television Wales and the West) in Wales, started to suffer serious financial losses. Enter James Buchan as controller of programmes, who with his head and his heart in the right place started producing local and light entertainment shows that miraculously increased the popularity of the station and saw its ratings and advertising go sky-high. By the end of the 1960s, Grampian had a potential audience of a million viewers with 200 staff employed in Aberdeen and in its various outposts. Grampian Television had become an overnight success, adored by its viewers who not only lapped up the programmes coming from the big ITV companies, but who had a staggering affiliation to the local material in a way that, even today, takes my breath away whenever I think about it. If big things come in small packages, then Grampian Television Ltd certainly earned its stripes and James Buchan, leading a comparatively small production team, brought success and high ratings envied by programme controllers far and wide, and smiles to the faces of investors.

***

One month into my new staff job with Grampian and I was not a happy man. Firstly, the station was smaller than I initially expected and that somewhat parochial Scottish, north-eastern atmosphere was not immediately palatable. I could barely understand the Doric – the broad north-eastern dialect, which when spoken at speed was unbelievably indecipherable. Douglas Kynoch, Grampian's very first continuity announcer, in his two interesting books, *Doric for Swots* and *Doric Proverbs and Sayings*, gives some excellent examples:

> There cam a day, fin Arthur fun his queen, the Leddy Grimavere, sittin her leen in her bed-chaamer, leukin rale doon-i-the moo. "Fit like?" speirt the keeng. Grimavere niver said naething. "Fit's the matter? He says. Hiv ye tint a shullin an fun a saxpence?" Syne, Grimavere halt ooy her hunkie an dabbit her een. "Leave's aleen," she said. "Fit wye?" says the keeng. "Fit ails ye, queen-quine? Yer face is fair trippin.

The English version would be:

There came a day when Arthur found his queen, the Lady of Guinevere, sitting alone in her bed-chamber, looking rather disconsolate or down-in-the-mouth. "How are you?" asked the king. Guinevere said nothing. "What's the matter?" he said. Have you lost a shilling and found a sixpence?" Soon, Guinevere drew out her handkerchief and dabbed her eyes. "Leave me alone," she said. "Why's that?" said the king. "What's wrong with you, my queen? You're so long in the face."

***

No one had been told about this new chap from Wales and I felt bewildered by the politics and smallness of it all: the language and culture brought no joy and the sheer distance, in miles, from the towns and cities I had always known was well beyond a few hours' travel. On the labour front, I was acclimatised to the larger television company and Grampian was certainly not fitting that bill. The studio and offices had been built where the old Aberdeen city tram shed had been; in fact, around the back of the building the tram shed was still there, housing the carpentry and paint shop for the building of sets, and a place for staff to park their cars.

Aberdeen itself, or 'Aiberdeen' if you are a true Scot, seemed decidedly rural in character. Even the streets that wound down to the boisterous North Sea were reminiscent of old *Boys' Own* sea shanties and reminded me of that painting of Sir Francis Drake as a boy, listening, spellbound, to the old sailor sitting on the upturned basket telling tales of sea adventures with pirates, buried treasure, and undiscovered islands far away.

Aberdeen, called the granite city, or the Britain in Bloom, best city, because of its amazing floral displays in parks and public places, is a sizeable place with two universities and many other notable institutions. Traditionally it was known for its deep-sea fishing port, its textile and paper industries. Its granite had been quarried from the Rubislaw Quarry, situated within the city, for well over 300 years and went into the building of the city itself and into the terraces of the Houses of Parliament and Waterloo Bridge in London. Today, Aberdeen is the city of so many things, including North Sea oil deposits, agriculture and soil research, and electronic design. Say what you like about the canny Scot, Aberdeen is a growing economy under the watchful eye of many city officials, but in the mid 1960s, real economic growth was still at grass-roots level and deep-sea fishing continued as it had done for years before.

Why did I feel like a fish out of water? The people were friendly but I could not engage with them. The studio audiences milled around like a market-day crowd, getting in the way of cameras and artistes. I was malfunctioning, feeling detached and depressed, unresponsive and friends with no one in particular. I was also missing Annette and her family and she and I would spend hours on the telephone each evening talking over the problems. My landlady and her husband were lovely people but, oh dear, conversing with them was another matter. I could not understand a single word they uttered and when they both argued with each other like a couple of machine guns, I felt like an interloper in outer Siberia:

"It's the hicht o bad manners an greed tae tak butter an jam on a biscuit."

"Ach, dinna fash yirsel, woman. Ye're lik coo in a driff."

Or put in plain English:

"It's the height of bad manners to put butter and jam on a biscuit!"

"Ah stop fussing yourself, woman. You are like a cow in a drift."

One night I faced the truth. I knew very little about the workings of a television station – just about the workings of a studio floor – and there was a great deal more to the industry than that. What did I know about cameras, studio lighting and sound, television graphics, design and the administration? Nothing! I knew little about creating television programmes and had shown little aptitude towards the job generally. It was time I faced reality and Grampian Television was the place to do it. They had been generous offering me a job; it was time I made an effort and showed some real gratitude and enthusiasm. I would find out how television really worked from all departments, not just on my own patch. More importantly I would learn about people; I would work with a whole range – from priests and cooks to all-in wrestlers, doctors, comics and entertainers. I would meet the technicians who made television pictures happen and meet people of great integrity and humour. I remember, Charles Smith, the head of news and current affairs saying to me that if I wanted to work on drama, best to go and start in the newsroom – there is plenty of drama there. The words stuck.

Three of the journalists in the newsroom, who went on to achieve national status, were good colleagues of mine at Grampian: the late talented and gentle voiced Donald (or Donnie) B. McLeod from Stornoway, Isle of Lewis, who became presenter of *Pebble Mill at One* in Birmingham; Graham Roberts, an announcer, actor and voice-over artiste of enormous skill eventually went to work for Yorkshire Television and took up a permanent position on *The Archers*, playing the gamekeeper, George Barford, for the next 31 years; the late Donald McCormick, who knew how to interrogate Scottish MPs with the teeth of a terrier, ended up presenting *Tonight, Newsnight, Question Time* and the *Money Programme* for the BBC. Grampian Television was a family affair for those who worked it and those who watched it; it also provided a solid starting point for those who wanted to move on in their careers.

***

The studio was in darkness. Five circular podiums were placed at various points on the floor and the spot lights would come up on each to reveal a different singer who would break into song. It was morning rehearsal and the singers were not arriving until the afternoon. Eddie Joffe, the producer/director of the programme, was having his camera 'stagger-through', a rehearsal for everyone behind the scenes. Cameramen were making notes on their shot cards, which would later remind them of the shots that would be required of each of them during the show. The music started up and I decided to stand on each podium in turn so that cameras had something to focus on – it's difficult to shoot an empty black space, so standing there would give them a chance to frame the shot. I then decided to sing from the script, with, I hasten to add, the most appalling voice. As the music increased in tempo, each soloist joined in a chorus which had me jumping from one podium to the other. Everyone in the studio roared with laughter, as did Eddie Joffe and his PA, Elaine. Sound department laughed, cameramen were framing their shots with big, broad smiles, the scene boys were helpless in their seats and lighting and vision control engineers were curled up in hysterics. Eddie shouted something in my earphones about how this was the worst singing he had ever heard coming from Wales. It was a mad, mad moment. Studio floor protocol went to the wall and everyone laughed until the tears ran. The show that evening went like clockwork and I cherished my artistes and took great care of them. We all retired to the club in the tram shed after the show and the laughing continued yet again.

I was now attuning myself to the people, the humour and the culture that made that little studio in the north-east of Scotland ultra efficient, staggeringly professional in its work, but friendly and relaxed enough to almost call itself a 'family concern'. It was unique in the ITV Network and in the coming years of my career, I would spell that out to people unequivocally, time and time again.

***

The light entertainment shows like the *Cairngorm Ski Night* was only one example of Grampian's success. The format was a simple one, but its effectiveness in attracting a studio audience and drawing in the viewers was a lesson in media marketing. A Scottish dance band led by the inimitable maestro and leader, Alex Sutherland, a collection of Scottish entertainers, singers, comedians, dancers, plus, and here was the magic ingredient, a hundred audience members, dressed in tartan and ready to take to the floor to dance and whoop till midnight. There was free beer on tap, wine, cheese and grapes, and an atmosphere brimming over with Scottish bonhomie. James Buchan, our programme controller, had encouraged his producers to capture the very essence of traditional Scotland with its throbbing, foot-tapping vibrancy, or with its lonely, Highland heroic ballads and laments. There were reels and jigs and all manner of country dances. Add to this the harps, fiddles, accordions, drums, bagpipes, whistles and piano – in fact, audience and studio crew alike would be so swept up with the emotion of the evening that it took a minute or two outside in the cold, crisp air to acclimatize oneself and return to the real world of roads and pavements and traffic. Directly opposite the studio was a taxi company that must have made a fortune on the backs of the happy and jovial crowds that came pouring out of that studio late at night, three times a week. There were the Hogmanay programmes and the Bill McCue shows: Bill with his rich, warm, bass baritone voice, an opera singer, actor and entertainer and a great friend of Welsh opera singer, Sir Geraint Evans.

Then there was *Calum's Céilidh*, featuring Calum Kennedy with that irrepressible glint in the eye and voice that could tap into all the powerfully emotive Scottish Highland and Gaelic songs. Calum was born, like journalist Donald MacLeod, on the Isle of Lewis, and married Anne Gillies, also a popular Gaelic singer. He was the father of five daughters, one of whom, Fiona, would partner him in song in later life. In 1957, Calum won the World Ballad Championship in Moscow, collecting his award from Russian leader, Nikita Khrushchev. In 1955 he had won the gold medal at the Scottish Mod in Aberdeen. Much of his singing was pure populist, with numbers like 'The Skye Boat Song' and 'Donald Where's Yer Troosers', but his Gaelic love songs were beautifully rendered and his 'Dark Lochnagar', Lord Byron's tribute to his childhood in Aberdeen, will go down in Scottish musical history as possibly his very best. Calum, for me, was a joy to work with and the only Scot to get me to wear a kilt.

Then came the Bothys!

The what, I hear you cry. *Bothy Nichts.*

Life was tough on the farmlands of north-east Scotland before the First World War. *Bothy Nichts* was a weekly programme which recreated those times on the land when farm labourers produced their own entertainment in a bothy which was a farm outhouse.

Grampian Television recreated this event as a weekly competition whereby a team of people would come onto a designed studio set resembling an old bothy and sit and entertain each other with traditional folk songs accompanied by violins, accordions, tin whistles and even elastic bands. There would be feats of skill and strength, but the emphasis was usually on music. Each group had a name: The Angus Cronies, The Fife Yokels, The Bennachie Sclabdadders and The Kennethmont Loons and Quines. The songs were traditional but popular: 'The Wee Cooper o' Fife', 'My Ain Wee Hoose', 'Auld Maid in the Garret', 'Maggie Cockabend' and many others. Each team was judged at the end of the series and a winning team announced. During my first week on the bothy I was totally flummoxed, for most of the language was broad Doric. I was soon indoctrinated and became totally intoxicated by this weekly event. As the photograph will testify, I made some wonderful friendships with the teams.

At the end of my first year at Grampian, a box arrived at Christmas containing a bottle of quality whisky – a gift from musical publisher, Boosey and Hawkes, and their representative, Mr Bassett Silver. What a wonderful name and such a generous man. His introduction usually started with the words, "Good morning. I'm the Boosey in Boosey and Hawkes!" I had been using their music alongside music from other television music publishers on all the mute films we ran on our daily news programme. Somehow, the gesture happily endorsed my decision to stay with Grampian and confirmed the development of another skill – that of finding and caring about the right choice of music to accompany a moving image. It was a skill that remained with me for the rest of my career.

Grampian Television made an abundance of local programmes in the late 1960s and I worked on every one of them. In total we had minimal staffing and quite likely the smallest of budgets. We all worked together on everything. We were all young. We were all learning. It was television production at grass-roots level and at its most creative. It was also in "the place where the typhoid came from", and I had every reason to stay.

CHAPTER 12

Morning Rolls and Forfar Bridies

I WAS IN a 'headlock' and there was no release. Saturday afternoon wrestling on ITV, with Kent Walton doing the commentary, brought its own brand of celebrities. George Kidd, five foot, six inches, lightweight wrestling champion of the world was demonstrating for us his 'locks' and 'holds' that had made him a global institution. In addition to his skill and tenacity, outside the ring, George became the Grampian Television Personality of the Year, and *The Wednesday People* programme, which he presented in the studio live every Wednesday was highly watchable. Nothing was demanded of him other than to sit on the edge of a table and read from a mini-cue which was a small box sitting over the camera lens containing his typed pieces to camera. So convincing was his cheeky-chappy delivery that the programme became yet another number one hit for the channel. George spoke the bits between the films which had been shot around the region, and were mostly light-magazine stories.

George Kidd was a consummate professional. He always appeared in the studio looking immaculate, dressed in an expensive suit but worried about his delivery of the lines. "Am I all right, David? Was that all right?" "How did I look, Hector?" he would address Hector the cameraman. He needed constant re-assurance and when we were showing a film clip and the studio would relax, I would rehearse his pieces to camera with him, operating the sewing machine button that moved the words at his reading speed in the mini-cue machine. George was on a live television show but, like in the wrestling ring, his performance had to be perfect. After we came off air, he would relax, buy everyone a drink in the club and move towards me grinning, "Shall I show you a couple of 'throws', David?" I'd back away, with a worried look on my face, although George really was a gentle giant when it came to demonstrating his skills to boys in the studio.

"Eh, no thanks, George. I leave all that to you."

***

I worked the daily news with Jimmy Spankie, a newsreader, continuity announcer, presenter, commentator, interviewer and a man from an influential family of jute merchants from Dundee. Jim was a well-known, front-of-camera performer who was as calm on the inside as he looked on the outside. Nothing rattled him and under the pressure of lights, microphones and cameras, his performance is impeccably relaxed and professional. All hell could be breaking loose around him and the programme falling to pieces but Jimmy would remain 'in control' and nothing would distract him from the job in hand. By the local viewing public, he was known as 'Spankie of the Grampian', a custodian of calmness which I was, unintentionally, about to put to the test.

We were in a cramped room which was effectively the continuity studio, the place where the announcer sat and appeared between programmes telling us what was coming up next. From here we were producing the live daily lunchtime and evening news and I was cramped on the floor, under the camera but within Jimmy's eye-line. I always gave him a cue to start speaking and to indicate that the camera was live and we were on air. The opening music started and finished, the camera light came on and I cued Jimmy by flicking my wrist forward under the lens but, the tubing inside my Biro developed a life of its own and went sailing past Jimmy's nose and slammed against the glass wall with a resounding clink that sent me rolling on the floor in silent mirth, with Jimmy trying to keep a straight face in front of the camera. I could just imagine the incident happening in slow motion. But do you know what? He didn't flinch and just kept reading on to the end of the bulletin, even though he was almost bursting to break into laughter himself. Jimmy and I, over the course of time, would become the firmest of friends, as did all the people I worked with in Grampian, but years later we would often laugh out loud at the Biro story.

Jimmy came to my aid on the accommodation front and offered me rooms in his beautiful town house, constructed of solid Aberdeen granite. The house was always full of laughter in those days and people would call and parties would be held, with debates and discussions continuing long into the night. Jimmy would come downstairs in the morning in his dressing gown and slippers and I would say, "Sleep well Jim?" He would say, "Like a log." And I would say, "Woke up in the fireplace?" He would then follow, "Feeling grate" (great). And we would then laugh and chorus, "Having spent a night on the tiles!"

Back at work, and the studio was only a stone's throw from his house, Jimmy and I would entertain the studio audiences before the recording. I would get them laughing by telling a few jokes to relax them and then introduce Jim, a former piper with the Black Watch, who would enter the studio to great applause playing the bagpipes. The audience would go wild with a thunderous welcome. There would be dancing and clapping and shouting and whooping and, whilst everyone was at fever pitch, a cameraman in some corner of the studio would train his lens on the old wooden clock that identified the programme. "Start the Clock," the director would call in my earphones, and there would be a minute's worth of clock recorded whilst I stood the band ready, with Jimmy dabbing his forehead of perspiration in some other corner of the studio

140

ready to deliver his opening piece to camera. In the middle of such merriment, the director would shout, "Cue the Band," and the boys would strike up and the viewers would feel that they had just opened the door on an amazing party and they just had to stop washing the dishes or hoovering the floor and sit back and watch the telly. Every week, our programme controller had at least four, if not, five programmes in the region's ratings of the top ten of television programmes.

There was *Cooking with Katie* with Katie Stewart, where a smaller studio was designed to look like Katie's kitchen at home. Those familiar words, "... and here's one I cooked earlier today", had the crew smacking their lips in anticipation of a great lunch. Why enjoy lunch at the staff canteen when Katie was serving up cordon bleu in the studio?

There was *Living and Growing* – a series on sex education for schools – a first for the ITV Network. Grampian was also the first of the ITV stations to show *Sesame Street*. There was news, current affairs, sport and programmes for farmers, programmes for young children at home and Grampian's own pop show, called *Pop Scotch*, with famous groups and soloists of the time: Lulu, Cilla Black, Peter Sarsted, Marmalade, Cat Stevens, Alan Price, Deep Purple and Hot Chocolate. We had programmes dealing with history and historical characters and even programmes on what the Christian newspapers were saying. Adam Faith came to the studio to take part in a discussion, and he offered me one of his cigars after the show. Prime Minister Harold Wilson came in with his customary pipe and made us all smile on the countdown to the start of the programme by looking up at me and saying, "It's a bit like Cape Canaveral in here!" Scottish MPs came and went – all to take part in *Points North*, a weekly political programme. Donald Dewar, a native of Glasgow who had won the Aberdeen South seat in 1966, would come in. He was, in my opinion, a Rottweiler in discussion and debate and went on to become, under Labour, Secretary of State for Scotland and then First Minister of Scotland in the newly-created Scottish Parliament.

Under his statue today in Glasgow are the words from the Scottish Act, 'There Shall Be A Scottish Parliament', to which Dewar himself, when looking at his image in stone, uttered the famous words, "I like that."

There were two other politicians I remember meeting in the studio at that time. One was Winifred 'Winnie' Ewing, a solicitor from Glasgow who moved into politics and won the watershed Hamilton by-election as the Scottish National Party (SNP) candidate. It seems that MPs are remembered as much for their famous utterances as their deeds in Parliament and at the time of her election, Winnie Ewing famously said, "Stop the world, Scotland wants to get on."

The other MP I remember meeting in 1969 was the Conservative MP for Aberdeenshire West, namely, Lieutenant-Colonel Colin Campbell Mitchell. Mentioned in dispatches, he became known as 'Mad Mitch' and, in 1967, led the Argyll and Sutherland Highlanders who attacked and reoccupied a crater in Aden. He was a high-profile, iconic figure, a smart and disciplined dresser and answered presenter Charles Smith's questions in a no-nonsense style.

This was repertory television and the best training ground for anyone entering the profession. It taught us speed, efficiency, an eye for detail and patience with people. Not unlike a repertory theatre, it was a question of preparing it, rehearsing it and recording it. And if we couldn't record, the programme went live. None of the stuff was edited, apart from film. There was no video tape editing and no dubbing. Commentaries, music and sound effects were played in live from the studio, not, as today, pre-recorded and added to the programme in a modern post-production editing and dubbing suite. Everything was transmitted in black and white on VHF 405 lines from the studio, a long way removed from high definition pictures on flat screens with programmes receiving post-production refinements prior to transmission.

**

Annette and I were married in Orpington in 1967 and spent our honeymoon travelling up the west coast of Scotland and then back down the east coast to Aberdeen. We moved to a new house some eight miles out of the city but close enough to the spectacular countryside of Royal Deeside. Melanie was born in 1971 – a little redhead who brought all the joys we could have wished for. My skin started playing up again and so did my eyes, leading to treatment for ulcers on my cornea – a repeat of an old problem that had started when I was very young. Childhood conjunctivitis and corneal ulcers plagued me for years. This time the skin on my body was so badly affected that the hospital insisted I wore miles of coal-tar-soaked bandages under my clothes. Under the lights of the studio I almost melted but never let on to anyone.

***

Between the pressures there was always laughter. I bought a Ford Anglia – our first family car. Taking it for a spin one Sunday afternoon, one of the tyres sustained a puncture. What did I do? After replacing it, I threw the tyre, complete with wheel, into a hedge. I told the lads the following morning what I had done, feeling quite proud of the fact that I had dealt with the matter promptly. Dare I say the laughter continued for weeks afterwards.

Eddie Joffe remembers the time he had some spring lambs on his programme. One of them decided to urinate over my shoes during rehearsal. When Eddie asked the reason for the delay, I went over to the boom microphone and uttered the words, "… this bloody lamb has pissed all over my Hush Puppies." The studio and gallery roared and collapsed with laughter. Eddie continues to remind me of the incident right up to the present day.

To Eileen, one of our production assistants, I was the man with the golden voice and she would say in rehearsal, "David, say my name again for me please." And I would again amble up to the boom and say, "Hello Eileeeeeen." Eileen would go all of a quiver and say, "Ahhhhhh... it's my Prince of Wales!" And there would be such laughter. Our friendship remains to this day and every Christmas, my card arrives from Scotland with 'My Prince of Wales' printed on the envelope, signed by Eileeeeen! All these people were the best to be with, all wonderfully creative and solid friends for life. There is no doubt that they all added in great measure to the success of Grampian Television in north-east Scotland.

Finally, two other names deserve my greatest respect and admiration. Jane and Alan Franchi. Hosts extraordinaire! These are the people who invented the true Scottish welcome. The door of their house was always open to friends and relatives. Jane would make the most enticing food and both knew the art of entertaining and making others feel special. They both did some amazing things in television. Jane worked for the BBC in Scotland and reported on the Piper Alpha oil platform disaster and on the fateful aircraft explosion over Lockerbie. Her network reports on these disasters will remain in the archives of Scottish social and broadcast history for ever. As for Alan Franchi... we met one day as he washed his Mini Cooper in the tram shed behind the studio.

Alan Franchi was a gentleman. Quietly spoken, a great sense of humour, a twinkle in the eye and devastatingly handsome with a thick mop of dark, floppy hair that he kept pushing out of his face. He was a true professional and was always dissecting arguments, initiating debates, and giving us an alternative way of looking at things. Alan was eventually offered a programme director's job and what a wonderful director he turned out to be. Doing a series of quiz programmes one afternoon, he asked me to floor manage and do the voice-overs, introducing the contestants from behind the scenery as they stepped forward to meet Lesley Blair, the quiz mistress. "You have a fine Welsh voice, David," he used to say, "It must be heard on air." I spent more time scripting what I was going to say on air than I did floor managing the show.

Cardiff and Bristol news presenters meet up at the Severn Bridge crossing. L–R: Mike Lloyd-Williams, Gwyn Llewelyn and Bruce Hokin.

With Sylvia Horne in the newsroom

A well-earned break in Bulawayo

A fledgling programme director in the early 1970s working on *Y Dydd* (The Day)

SOUND ON
VISION ON
REHEARSAL

A sign advising silence outside the old studio 2 in Pontcanna

Me directing Gwyn Parry at Taff's Well in 1974, with cameraman Tony Impey

Filming in Zimbabwe, under constant watch by the military

At last I get to stand with the crew on the Hollywood Walk of Fame. The famous Manns Chinese Theatre is in the background.

With film cameraman John Williams in Israel

The 1980s – graves at the Berlin Wall, celebrations for President Mugabe in Zimbabwe, and filming at Sharp Electronics in Japan

My growing family between global locations

With fellow producers in the House of Commons: me, Ronw Protheroe, the late Peter Elias Jones and the late Owen Griffiths

Richard Burton was filming *Wagner* in Switzerland when HTV Wales invited him to London to play in a stage version of Dylan Thomas's *Under Milk Wood*. An interview with the great man was not to be missed. I stand to the right of Burton among crew and HTV management: John Morgan left, David Meredith behind him, Geraint Talfan Davies front row right.

The happiest of shoots on *Tomorrow's Star Maybe*, outside London's Victoria Palace

Little Suzie Kemys from Cwmbrân who played a stint as *Annie* at the Victoria Palace in London, 1980s

The three little *Annie* orphans at the stage door: Helen Thorne, Suzie Kemys and Catherine Zeta Jones

Courtesy ITV Wales / National Library of Wales

Me (back right) with three wonderful ladies from *West End Girls*: Suzie, Helen and Catherine

Courtesy of ITV Wales

Julius Tengler, Luftwaffe bomb aimer over Pembroke Dock, Swansea and Cardiff, 1940–5, stands left. Crew in the middle and programme advisors on the right.

Courtesy ITV Wales / Western Telegraph / National Library of Wales

Poignancy of graphic 'Inferno' film

Pembroke Dock women who recognised their fathers amongst the rescuers at Pembroke Dock in *War Over Wales.*

Courtesy ITV Wales / *Western Telegraph* / National Library of Wales

Timothy West with a great little Welsh train in *Engine Whistle Blowing*, 1980s

Courtesy of ITV Wales / National Library of Wales

Alan Rustad, journalist, presenter, co-producer and friend. A joy to work with.

HTV's new television headquarters at Culverhouse Cross in Cardiff in the early 1980s

Success, the opening night launch programme shows the enormity of the main studio

Marketing and promotion of *Telethon '88*. Idwal Symonds, chief executive on the left; stalwarts Ruth Madoc and Arfon Haines Davies, presenters; Jane Thomas, fundraiser; myself and Emyr Daniel, controller of programmes.
Courtesy ITV Wales

A talented line-up for my front-of-camera team on *Telethon '88*, led by the indefatigable Arfon Haines Davies (far right) who knew how to fill the space when the going got tough. With Arfon, some equally amazing trailblazers: L–R Roy Sheppard, Owen Money (now MBE), Ruth Madoc and Aled Jones.
Courtesy ITV Wales / National Library of Wales

"Our guest tonight is from the Monopolies Commission who are investigating over-manning in television."

Sadly the Mac cartoon in the *Daily Mail* had it right. With job losses, tears and heartbreak, the dismantling and restructuring of ITV was to take place on a grand scale throughout the 1990s.

© Mac, *Daily Mail*

With all the cutbacks, I was now heading Features and Community Programme departments and still making my own programmes as a researcher, producer, director, presenter, and journalist. Interviewing – once done by journalists – was an everyday occurrence.

Two of the many interview set-ups for *The Really Helpful Programme*

The small dedicated team for *The Really Helpful Programme*
Courtesy ITV Wales

A proud moment – presenter Sara Jones and I collect our *Really Helpful Programme* award
Courtesy ITV Wales

Looking as brown as berries, shooting the *Royal Welsh Show Special* with cameraman Martin Duckett. Presenter / journalist Mike Lloyd-Williams bringing up the rear.

Rovi, the Welsh magician on the *Elinor* programme

Shooting in Japan

The Japanese welcome in the Sharp Electronics boardroom in Osaka

Suitable protection from the Israeli sun perhaps? I don't think so!

A muddy field in Bethlehem

From faraway places (Japan and Israel) to filming the Tal-y-Llyn railway in the beautiful Snowdonia foothills

Time to reflect. Back home in Aberystwyth.

Before Alan's days as a programme director we had both been floor managing for a couple of years and then one day an internal memo arrived for each of us that was to shake us to the core. Only by sharing the problem would we survive and live to see another day.

Would you please undertake acting responsibility as programme director on the undernoted dates:

3 September	Police News/Action News
10 September	*Romper Room*
15 September	Good News for Modern Man

Thank you
James Buchan

My legs started to wobble with nerves. There must be some mistake. Alan confirmed my suspicions and went upstairs to query it with Jim's secretary. He came back down and said there was no mistake. Floor managers were expected to direct when the staff directors were not available. Please, please, let something happen to change Jim's mind and get me off the hook. There was another problem. We had to do our own vision mixing, in other words, sitting in front of a huge panel of buttons cutting to the right camera at the right time or cutting to the film or cutting to... whatever else we had to cut to but, HELLS BELLS! – this was not for me.

Alan and I pressed our noses to the gallery window, watching the other directors at work; all supremely calm and confident. I hardly slept and what would happen if I cocked the whole thing up and the programme was not good enough to transmit. We dreaded the thought and tried not to think about the dire consequences.

***

My first programme was *Police News* with WPC Moira Winchester. The crew around me were absolutely terrific;

they were all my friends and they must have guessed how I was feeling. To sit in that seat in the gallery was an awesome experience. The overhead lights were dimmed and we sat in semi-darkness under the simple strip lights that lit our script area. After the brightness of the studio, this felt very strange. Eileen, my production assistant or my 'Princess of Scotland', sat to my right.

Someone somewhere was waiting for me to say something, but my voice had disappeared down a mouth that was as dry as the Sahara desert.

"Are we going to hear those Welsh dulcet tones?" asked Donald on Camera 2.

"Are you there David?" asked Curly on Camera 1, zooming in and out on WPC Moira's badge which was glistening under the studio lights.

"We need to spray down the badge, Dave," someone said in Racks (Vision Control).

Then Norman, who was mixing the sound, looked through his glass panel and gave me a wave and said Sandy was adjusting the microphone on Moira's desk – could he have two minutes? I felt like saying, "Norman, you can take the rest of the day, I'm bloody terrified." It was a very strange experience listening to disembodied voices in the darkness, and when I did summon up the courage to say something, I felt more at ease. Had it not been for the warmth and support of the friendship around me, I doubt whether I would have managed that first programme. The hour passed like lightning.

"Hello studio, VTR here." The video tape recording department upstairs were checking the tape for any glitches in the picture.

"Yes, VTR," I said hesitatingly.

"Your programme is clear."

The words came through like music to my ears. I positively glowed with confidence.

"Thank you VTR. Thank you studio, thank you everyone."

I had forgotten about poor young WPC Moira Winchester

in the studio who had performed so admirably but Alan had, unfailingly, looked after her. I kept thanking the crew for days afterwards. I had directed my first television programme; it was only a ten-minute police bulletin about things lost or stolen in the area but it was my first, and I felt I was walking on air.

Alan Franchi spent the remainder of his career at Grampian Television and rose to become a highly-distinguished producer/director. His crowning achievement was directing on television, and then on stage, *Scotland the What?* – a trio of Aberdonians who had devised a comedy revue at university, taking a sly dig at Scotland and its culture. It was Alan who introduced *Scotland the What?* to the television studio and their name and brand of comedy became regional and national institutions through Alan's untiring efforts. He was an avid supporter of the Aberdeen Arts Centre and campaigned with courage and strength to successfully keep the centre open. Alan died in August 2010, aged 81, and Jane, whom he married in 1975, survives him. We lost a very dear friend from the industry and one I shall never forget.

***

We formed our own Grampian Drama Society; nothing for transmission, but for showing live on stage to Aberdeen audiences. I had already been part of one group in the city and had played one of the junkie brothers in *A Hatful of Rain* – a rather grim story of an American family in Brooklyn living with a drug problem. According to the local newspaper, my performance '... was impressive but with an American accent that came and went!' I was never very good at accents. This was followed by, *Boeing-Boeing,* a comedy starring two friends who do a fine line in air hostesses. But it was *The White Sheep of the Family* that took all my energies. A comedy about a family of thieves, and I played the unsuspecting old vicar who has the best comic lines in the play. All these performances were on top of three late nights a week in the studio. It was a good feeling to be on stage again but with a great deal more security than I had experienced in the past. Father McGregor, a friendly Roman Catholic priest and one of Grampian's religious advisors, invited me to perform in a poetry and choral speaking evening with some local personalities. So there was never a dull moment and it was good to be giving live performances again.

I worked with Grampian Television in Aberdeen for five years and, during that time, bought a house and started a family. I also made a connection with Scotland that has never left me and when I learned that my ancestors on my father's side had come from Dumfries and walked to west Wales with their animals, I was not a bit surprised. In my dreams I would like to think that those ancestors had strong links with the north-east – who's to know?

The floor managing continued and my self-inflicted popularity with studio audiences, warming them up and introducing them to Jimmy Spankie, became a feature three times a week. We had developed such an act in studio warm-ups that one evening some ladies in the audience presented me with a bag of Forfar Bridies, a kind of north-eastern pasty from Forfar, which were delicious to eat, and morning rolls were given to me by the bucketful – they being a kind of salted breakfast bread roll, delicious with butter and marmalade and usually called 'rowies'. Jimmy also became godfather to Melanie, our first daughter.

In September 1971, the coming of colour to Grampian Television coincided with the company's tenth anniversary. The studio cameras were large, grey cumbersome things with black and white viewfinders, but the pictures they produced were in breathtaking colour, and after years of 405 line black and white pictures, 625 lines with colour was like coming out into the sunshine. The studio was warmer, with increased candle power from the lights. Make-up on faces became more precise and any little smudges on scenery or on studio props and furnishings were immediately noticed under the glare of higher quality pictures. Making-do and mending was now a thing of the past as higher-quality colour pictures showed up every blemish. There was much to celebrate, and the channel's anniversary and the advent of colour pictures brought out the best in all of us.

***

After nearly five years at Grampian Television it was time to move on and seek fresh opportunities. From Scotland I had seen the coverage of the catastrophic and tragic Aberfan disaster on TWW and some time later, the investiture of HRH The Prince of Wales in glorious black and white from the fledgling company called Harlech Television. This company had won the franchise to broadcast from TWW and it looked like a company with promise. I applied for a floor manager's job and the interview went well. I was Welsh and could call upon a great deal of experience in the industry. They offered me the job some weeks later and I approached Jim Buchan to seek his advice. Would he offer me the advertised programme director's job in Aberdeen, or should I go to live and work in Cardiff? This was a real dilemma and only Jim Buchan could help me with it. He had always been straight with me and it was only fair I spelt out my situation to him.

Jim assured me that I had put in some splendid work for Grampian Television, but he had decided to give the programme director's job to someone else with more experience in that field. He also felt that Wales was where I had come from and that it was only natural that I should return there, to a company that was large and enterprising enough to develop and expand my skills. He followed this up by saying that I would be sadly missed. I thanked him warmly for offering me five very rewarding years of work.

My farewell party was an outrageously drunken affair but tinged with all the sadness one feels when leaving friends and not really knowing when one was going to see them again. Our house was sold to an oil company and Aberdeen was about to change. The discovery of North Sea oil saw to that. Annette and Melanie had already flown south. My head, the morning after my leaving party, was throbbing and as heavy as lead. It was time, however, to say my final farewells. I was travelling south by overnight train that evening and had a sleeping compartment booked to King's Cross in London and then on to Cardiff.

***

The Northern lights of Aberdeen are what I long to see
The Northern lights of Aberdeen, that's where I long to be.

So in 1972 it was time to leave my beloved Scotland. The train drew out of the station and the platform slipped away revealing the Aberdeenshire countryside and the wild beautiful coastline. I whispered the words of a song that I had heard so many times in the studio and it had come to mean so much. I reflected: maybe I was a true Scotsman. I felt like one after five years in Aberdeen. My mind was made up. I was a true Welshman with Scottish blood flowing through my veins.

I've been a wanderer all of my life and many a sight I've seen,
God speed the day when I'm on my way to my home in Aberdeen.

The same could be said of Aberystwyth, of course. Both places hung on my shoulders like well-worn pullovers. Aberystwyth with its echoes of my teenage and adolescent years and Aberdeen, the granite city, with its people who carved their culture and friendship upon my soul. If Aberystwyth had given me a good start, Aberdeen, without hesitation, trained and developed my early career in preparation for the job that lay ahead for me.

Seagulls swooped over the cliffs of that wild Scottish territory as the train under a late evening sky tore its way southward towards Edinburgh and northern England. I was leaving home and going home – if you see what I mean. Back to Wales but back to what? This time I knew the answer. Scotland had seen to that. I sat back in my seat, lit a cigarette and gazed hypnotically out at the rushing countryside. It was beginning to rain. It knew how to rain in Aberdeen. In sunshine, the granite buildings gleamed; in rain, it adopted a greyness that clung. The muffled clatter of the train's wheels sent me slowly to sleep as my mind drifted over the past and towards a future full of the old uncertainties.

CHAPTER 13

Men of Harlech

HTV WAS RUN by giants: Lord Harlech, Wynford Vaughan-Thomas, John Morgan, Sir Geraint Evans, Stanley Baker, Richard Burton, Sir Alun Talfan Davies. All these men were learned and influential and they came from Wales. Their fields of expertise covered medieval history, politics, law, journalism, broadcasting, music, opera and acting. The original consortium was minus a chairman and when Lord Harlech was invited, a man whose family background stretched back to Welsh antiquity, here was a group that carried a high degree of pedigree.

Why TWW (Television Wales and the West) lost its franchise to broadcast in 1967 was the subject of much conjecture. They had been operating successfully for ten years and numerous reasons were given for their demise, ranging from political to domestic. Whatever the reason, when I was appointed to join the staff in 1972, HTV had already been in operation for nearly four years in Wales and the West Country. The letters, HTV were a substitute for Harlech Television, a choice heartily applauded by our cousins across the Severn estuary. I recall the old Harlech Television logo; it reminded me of an advertisement for travel sickness, its animated, horizontal lines blurring the vision and making us all feel quite unsteady on our feet.

This was a company vastly different in size and vision from Grampian, but doubtless its revenue would have been greater when comparing the enormous size of the viewing population. Operating from the old TWW studios in Cardiff and Bristol, the company's initial task was to earn the loyalty of the viewers who felt displaced by the loss of TWW. HTV's other commitment was to run a comparable, yet different, service for viewers both sides of the estuary. Two boards of management were created, one in Cardiff, the other in Bristol. The viewers in Wales were divided yet again between those who preferred their programmes in English and those who wanted them in Welsh. It was a complicated situation but, unknowingly at the time, became the blue print for the creation, years later, of S4C – the Welsh fourth channel.

The problem of running a bilingual service soon became apparent. People in Cardiff were switching their roof aerials over to the Mendip transmitter, thereby eliminating the Welsh programmes altogether. The problem with that, however, was that it was eliminating all the HTV English language programmes from Wales as well. It was not uncommon to walk into a Cardiff chip shop and see customers waiting for their chips to fry watching the local news from Bristol. Efforts may well have been made to encourage the aerial erectors of Cardiff to ensure that ITV aerials faced the Wenvoe transmitter and not the one on the Mendip Hills. However, as far as the rest of Wales was concerned, viewers were stuck with the bilingual service whether they wanted it or not. In a cultural and political sense though, it was exposing the language to the non-Welsh speakers and that was not altogether a bad thing.

There was still great public confusion. One viewer thought the quality of the pictures looked better since the Harlech takeover despite the fact that no technical changes had been made. Another viewer rang up from the town of Harlech on the Welsh coast asking where in that town were the studios situated? He was disappointed to hear they were miles away in Cardiff. A third viewer turned up at the studios asking to see the horses featured in *Rawhide* with Clint Eastwood. It was explained to him by our esteemed public relations officer that the cowboy series was made in America and brought in by the British ITV Network: there were no horses or cowboys and Indians in Pontcanna. After a tour which lasted about an hour and, just as he was about to say goodbye, he turned to the press officer and said, "... but you still haven't shown me the horses from *Rawhide*." As far as the viewing audiences were concerned, everything was lumped together and made at our Cardiff studios.

HTV was big and ambitious. When I arrived in 1972, I learned they were making 'made-for-television' feature films for the English ITV Network and for the international market. *Arthur of the Britons*, *The Pretenders* and, in later years, *Robin of Sherwood*, *The Snow Spider* and *Return to Treasure Island* to name but a few amongst a whole plethora of others. HTV were fulfilling their obligations on all fronts but also providing that local service for viewers in two languages in Wales and one language in the West Country. Different cultures, different identities, bigger budgets, larger staff, greater revenues and programmes being made on an unprecedented scale, seven days a week. I had much to learn.

***

The first days in a new job are the worst and I was lost amongst people, many of whom had worked for TWW and still bore the wounds of having to be re-interviewed for their old jobs. Four years on and there was still ill-feeling towards the 'Daleks from Harlech' and sadness felt for those who had either decided to jump ship or were permanently dismissed.

There were at least ten programme directors, with an army of freelancers making their entrances and exits. There were a number of film crews out and about every day, with many electricians, an outside broadcast department, journalists, film editors, researchers, a dubbing theatre for adding commentaries, music and sound effects. The dubbing theatre itself had a floor that could be removed in squares to reveal an assortment of ground surfaces on which one could walk to emulate the sound of feet walking on gravel, on sand, through bracken, on pavements, in water or mud or snow. *Arthur of the Britons* and other such films made by HTV in the early days had numerous sword fights – all the sword clashes had to be added on in the dubbing theatre. When the series was sold to American television, each sword clash had to be re-done because the Americans liked their sword clashes to sound hard and metallic and with added echo. I recall an editor telling me that he had to lay the tracks for over 800 sword clashes on a complete series and then lay each one down in the dubbing theatre over the pictures. We take everything so much for granted when watching it on television. And what of *Shane* with Alan Ladd – that famous cowboy film bought by HTV and shown in the Welsh language? Another job for the dubbing theatre. I am uncertain to this day who voiced Alan Ladd and Jack Palance in Welsh. All that effort, all that skill, and all that hard graft in making something look and sound so realistic... and that is what I loved about the whole business of making television programmes.

There was overtime to be made: *Sion a Siân*, the equivalent of *Mr and Mrs* in Welsh – three programmes with an audience – were recorded on Saturday morning: eight hours at double time added nicely to my salary. I could not believe that I was being asked to work on a Saturday morning, but it was not unusual with HTV – there were so many programmes to record. There were musical programmes with Sir Geraint Evans, Welsh choirs and discussions; *Outlook* on Friday evenings – a studio-based current affairs discussion with Sir Alun Chalfont doing the interrogating. *Y Dydd* (The Day) and *Report Wales* went out nightly – 20 minutes of Welsh news followed by 20 minutes of English news with a commercial break in between.

There were numerous programmes in Welsh and in English: children's programmes, light entertainment and documentaries. There were outside broadcasts: horse racing, tennis, boxing, adventure documentaries with Leo Dickenson, church services, the National Eisteddfod, general elections, Royal and papal events. There were documentaries with Wynford Vaughan-Thomas, exploring everything from mountain tops, Welsh castles, waterways to coastline. Someone once said that Wynford had explored everything in Wales except Welsh sewers! He had climbed through every nook and cranny and was a wonderful contributor to our programmes. The late Emyr Daniel, who became managing director years later, once called Wynford Vaughan-Thomas 'a life enhancer' and he was absolutely right. He was a man who, as a BBC war correspondent in the 1940s, had witnessed the horrors of the Belsen concentration camp and, after that, never took life too seriously.

I was asked to floor manage the golf at St Pierre: it was even more of a joy when I discovered it was being directed by Hector Stewart of Central Television in Birmingham – my old friend from Grampian days. Hector had realised his dream and was now doing the big stuff immaculately and so professionally. The outside broadcast was technically enormous and complex, with several greens to be covered and Hector rose to the occasion magnificently.

The trade unions at ITV were all-powerful in those early days. We all paid our 'subs' and it was necessary to belong to a union otherwise there was no job. There were unions for scene shifters, electricians, journalists and technicians and it was this last category – the Association of Cinematograph Television and Allied Technicians (ACTT) – that was the most powerful and the one to which I belonged. It is fair to say that all the salary structures were based on negotiations between management and the unions and all rules of work were contained in 'the little white book'. If the ACTT made a complaint, management had to listen and sabres would be drawn and cages rattled until an agreement was reached. ITV was flourishing, and so were the unions contained within it. The problems came when loyalties were split but, in my career, that problem was some way off. It struck me as odd that management were always anxious you had an ACTT ticket before offering you a job. It would not have been in their interests to employ someone who was not a member of the union. I kept well away from such controversial matters and paid my subs!

***

During the early 1970s, HTV Wales and West produced advertising sketches called 'ad mags'. They were usually played out in the commercial breaks in between all the other advertisements and doubtless they were lucrative for the ITV companies that made them. If you are of the generation that remembers 'ad mags' on the television, you will recall the setting. They were little dramas, set usually in a kitchen where a neighbour would come in for a cup of tea and unload her shopping bags, telling Mrs So and So what she had bought. It was all so twee and cosy and jolly and the whole thing never lasted for more than two or three minutes, but they were a living hell to floor manage! A director from Bristol, who was well-versed in the shooting of 'ad mags', would come over to Cardiff and blast his way through the production. Here is a sample of what was said:

"Get that woman to hit those marks. If she doesn't put that Heinz Baked Bean tin down on the correct mark on the table, we are all snookered... and that Vesta Curry packet keeps overlapping the Cornflakes and Lux Soap. Tell 'em to hit their marks, David. And where's the drinking chocolate? For goodness sake, where is she putting the drinking chocolate? I don't want it behind the Heinz Salad Cream. The camera will never see it there. Tell her we have to see the label. Go again. Pleeeeze, God help me. Let's go again."

The actors would get themselves ready, one behind the kitchen door, ready to make her entrance on my cue, holding her bulging shopping basket. Cue Betty.

"Oh, hello Betty." (opening door and making an entrance)

"Hello Gwen."

"You have been busy, Betty. Where have you been?"

"I went down to the new Fine Fare on the corner, it's a smashin' new shop. Best in the valley."

"Really, what's it called again?"

"Fine Fare. There is something for everyone in Fine Fare."

"Oh really. What have you bought?"

"Well, first of all these baked beans are a real bargain. Only 20p a tin."

"Mmmmmm... lovely."

"... and the whole family love these new Vesta Curries... and as for the salad cream..."

"STOP! STOP! STOP!" shouts the director. "What is she doing? Camera 3, where are you going?"

The cameraman on Camera 3 replies, "I'm waiting for the Lux Soap. Is this where she puts it?" pointing his lens towards a spot on the table.

"We are all waiting for the bloody Lux Soap, darling. I'm coming out on the floor, David. Set it up from the beginning again and I will walk it through with them."

One day's work on 'ad mags' and you went home with a big headache. The Independent Television Authority finally put a stop to them. The director in question really was the best in the business for directing local advertisements. The last time, I recall, he had landed a major contract for HTV; making advertisements for a leading Sunday newspaper to be shown over the entire ITV network... but not in the style of the 'ad mag' I'm pleased to say.

**

At a large stately home, near Abergavenny, the lady in charge was under the impression that a small camera crew were going to turn up. You can imagine the look on her face when an outside broadcast unit turned up with a vehicle resembling a furniture removal truck with two other vehicles in attendance. Someone, somewhere, had not explained that an outside broadcast unit is, in reality, a studio on wheels and not unlike a travelling circus with large cameras, miles of cables, scaffolding, lights, microphones, prop and costume vehicles and 15 to 20 people.

Her mouth dropped even further when she saw lily pads growing on the lake fronting the house, and flowers and shrubs in full bloom, courtesy of designer and prop buyers. There was also a small cast of singers, all dressed in 18th-century skirts and breeches, frock coats, cornered hats and white gloves, and with live white poodle dogs.

Sir Geraint Evans was recording some musical pieces for two programmes, one in Welsh, the other in English. This was when I saw the true measure of a designer at work. This was a page from the history books, television aerials had been removed, paths and roads made to look rough and stony and the house and gardens just gleamed like something out of a Jane Austen novel. All the music and singing had been pre-recorded and was played back to the artistes as they mimed the words very convincingly, walking between shrubs and under rose-covered garden archways. Two stunt men came rolling down a wooden stairway leading to a barn, kicked out by the wench at the top of the stairs. Michael Roberts, our first assistant director, and I threw live chickens into the shot as the men hit the bottom of the stairs; someone else created a cloud of dust in front of the camera. By Take 3, the poor stunt men were feeling quite bruised. This entire sequence would be played over a verse from a song and all that would happen in editing at a later stage. It was a song about drunken, marauding peasants.

Sir Geraint Evans would have one particular man to hold what we called the 'idiot boards'. Not that Sir Geraint was an idiot, far from it, but the name 'idiot board' came from film industry history. It was basically a large prompt board on which we would print the words of the song which was being sung in large letters. Although the music itself had already been recorded, the board was a reassurance for Sir Geraint as he mouthed the words and strode over hill and dale. Frankie, our beloved wardrobe assistant was camp, gentle and loveable, and had enough to do assisting with all the 18th-century costumes and wigs. But, if Frankie was not standing alongside the camera holding the boards up for the great man, Sir Geraint would split the country asunder with his great bass-baritone voice, "F R A N K I E E E E E E," and running over the hill towards us would be Frankie in his flared trousers, high-heeled shoes, hair flowing in the breeze and a worried look on his face.

"I'm coming Sir Geraint, I'm on my way, honest I am."

In the pub that evening, we would all be laughing until tears ran and Frankie would look at me and say in all seriousness with that wonderful camp tone to his voice, "I don't mind dressing him, David, but why does he insist on me holding the idiot boards?"

I struggled to give him an answer.

"Because no one can do it as well as you, Frankie. No one," and we would laugh and drink until two in the morning.

One evening I entertained the crew with my magic or, rather, my mind-reading ability. With an accomplice sitting opposite me, I was able to tell the playing card that had been chosen by feeling for the number of taps I was receiving from my accomplice on my foot under the table. Unfortunately, everyone else had guessed the secret and about six pairs of feet were knocking me about the ankles; we collapsed in helpless laughter. On another occasion a group of us went into a sweet shop and started perusing the shelves. One of my colleagues came in and asked the shopkeeper behind the counter whether he had any chocolates with…? His mind went blank, he couldn't think of the word. "Nuts," exclaimed the shopkeeper, at which point the rest of us in the shop turned round and, copying the television commercial, chorused:

"Nuts, whole hazel nuts
Cadbury's make 'em and
They cover them in chocolate."

Fortunately for us, the shopkeeper had a great sense of humour and laughed with the rest of us. We explained who we were and what we were doing in the area. Boys will be boys!

160

***

Twelve months into my employment with HTV Wales, I applied for a programme director's job. Don't ask me why. Had Grampian given me a new confidence? It is highly possible. Nevertheless, I had several worries. I noticed that HTV directors put 'shot numbers' to everything. In other words, every camera shot taken by the director in the gallery was pre-planned and given a number. For English-speaking cameramen – and they were in the majority – shot numbers were essential on a Welsh programme: they would never have been able to understand what was coming up next without shot numbers. In Grampian, language was not an issue and cameramen had been so generous – they virtually offered the shots and I took them. HTV was a new discipline. Everything had to be pre-planned, right down to the most minute detail. There were planning meetings where everything would be spelt out. Directors would relate how they saw a particular scene going. These meetings were attended by design, lighting, cameras, sound, wardrobe, make-up, and scene crew foreman. Nothing was ever left to chance. I was confident I would not get the job; I had been there only a year and there were people on the staff who were more capable than me, having been there longer and being more experienced. I applied, underwent a reasonable interview with Aled Vaughan, the controller of programmes, and forgot the whole affair, for I was second assistant director on a major drama series for the ITV Network.

The Inheritors was written by Wilfred Greatorex who had, some years earlier, written *The Plane Makers* and *The Brothers* for television. *The Inheritors* was a six-part drama about a wealthy aristocratic, Welsh family who discover that a rich supply of oil lies beneath their vast acreage of land. Add to this plot all the intricacies of family life with love affairs, relationships, and legal battles and you will begin to get an idea of the series. All exteriors were to be shot on film at locations in Wales and London and the interiors would be recorded in the Cardiff studio. It was an immense undertaking for any regional company because it involved studio and location work, transportation, outside catering, actors with national status, huge quantities of equipment ranging from generators to supply our lighting needs, helicopters and day- and night-time shoots. There was sound and camera equipment, 'grips', another word used in the film industry to describe the railway lines or tracks that are laid on uneven roads and pavements for the camera to travel down, especially when the subject is moving. All this was in addition to the remainder of the technical paraphernalia, not forgetting make-up, wardrobe and props departments and hired vehicles which were to be driven by the actors. There were also low-loaders, a very low-to-the-floor form of transportation to carry an anchored motorcar with actors in the front seats and a complete camera crew, the actors seemingly giving the impression of driving themselves down the motorway when, in fact, they were being towed. Police co-operation was essential.

On a big film shoot like this, the director has a first assistant to organise the actors and crews and to bark the orders like a sergeant major. The director himself will direct quietly, chatting with his actors, explaining to the lighting cameraman and camera operator what he requires. I was assistant to the first assistant, Mike Roberts, who in my opinion, had the unit running like a well-oiled machine, pre-empting all the director's requirements and being one, if not two steps ahead of the director in setting up the shots. I would run for Mike, ensuring everybody knew the order of shooting sequences, particularly actors, who had a dreadful habit of wandering off, especially if we were in the grounds of Powis Castle or shooting in a busy retail store in the middle of London. We all stayed in a Shrewsbury hotel and Mike and I would be up at six in the morning giving morning calls to actors, making sure everyone was at breakfast and on that bus by 7.30 a.m. to take them to the first location which could be some miles out. There were restless moments, when we would have to tour the town looking for missing actors who had wandered off in the middle of the night. Mike was first assistant on the first block of filming and then we swapped for the second block. It was my first introduction to filming drama with all its many components. Scene by scene, shot by shot, everything took an interminable amount of time. There were re-takes and re-takes. Our wardrobe lady insisted Meredith Edwards was wearing the wrong jacket as he came out of that castle door in shot number 872, scene 64. In the studio, he had walked out of the baronial living room in a green jacket. On the location work, six weeks later, he was dressed in a Harris tweed. The director was told and he was fiercely cross but decided not to re-do the shot, we were too far ahead and losing time. We had to keep moving to avail ourselves of the daylight.

We also shot on the old Severn Bridge. I perched with the camera crew on the highest girder of the structure communicating with Mike Roberts lying on the floor of a red BMW cuing him on a 'walkie-talkie' radio. Phil Madoc and Sarah Douglas were in the front seats and they crossed the bridge. The director was unhappy with the shot for various reasons and we had to repeat it. I instructed Mike in the BMW who had to turn the car around at the next roundabout on the M4 and do the shot again – in fact we got the shot right in four takes. For all these sequences with the bridge and motorway there were unprecedented levels of safety precautions, but on that bridge cross-over girder, there was only a simple wire fence between me and infinity. I refused to look down.

Shooting in the middle of a London street was murderous with traffic, police, actors and crew. We also had to keep the public moving; they would stop and stare which made the shot very unreal. At the end of each shot, the gate in the camera was inspected. If there was a speck of dust in the film gate, we had to repeat the shot. Every evening, the 'rushes' were sent off by dispatch rider to a processing laboratory in London. We were informed the following morning whether or not the negative was looking good. If it was not, everything had to be shot all over again which is why every care was taken to keep the inside of the camera clean and free from dust; even film stock was changed inside a black bag to keep daylight well away.

Tony Impey was one of the country's finest cinematographers. I watched him light a London alleyway at night using 'brutes' – enormous arc lamps which worked off a generator. He created a natural night-time light with even a touch of moon-glow as we followed our actors, a male and female, out of a tucked-away London restaurant and down a cobbled alleyway. The couple stopped and chatted and kissed in a doorway. The interior of the restaurant would be done in the studio in a month's time but the exterior of the London alleyway at night looked amazing and so natural. We started work at 6.30 p.m. and finished at midnight. For a sequence that lasted 45 seconds in the edited film, literally hours of work were spent in creating it. The reason everything was shot out of order was because of so many variables. The weather, the availability of actors, the use of locations. It would be wasteful to shoot in one location, leave it and then return to it a week later. Best to do all the sequences that were called for in that alleyway on that night when we had the required permission, rather than return there with all that equipment a week later. Everything was logistically worked out.

Alan Franchi, my friend in Grampian was shooting a sequence with Richard Clayderman, the celebrity French pianist many years later in a Scottish castle. They had hired the piano at some expense and when it was returned to the owner three days later, Alan suddenly remembered he wanted some medium close-ups of Richard playing – just head and shoulders. So they sat Richard at a table, played the music back to him on loud speakers. He pretended to play the piano but was in fact playing the table! Meanwhile, some visitors were being shown round the castle and were amazed to look through a window and see Mr Richard Clayderman playing a table and producing the most amazing music!

***

I was up to my eyes in the studio on the last week of recording interior sequences. Mike was running the floor and I told him that I was just slipping out to 'check the horses', or go to the loo! I was in the gents when in walked the company personnel officer.

"Ah David... congratulations. You are our new trainee programme director. Written confirmation will be sent to you this afternoon."

He left and I stood alone for a few minutes thinking it through. After having survived so many twists and turns in my career, it took some time for the news to penetrate. I had once been such a low achiever with equally low self-esteem. My life in work had been a bumpy ride with struggle and misfortune but, somehow, I had come through all that and been given a job that years ago would have been beyond my wildest dreams. I went to the reception area and rang Annette and my mother and father with the wonderful news. It was all more than I had ever hoped for.

I was now a television programme director, my mind traced the journey and I was elated and overjoyed. When I broke the news to the cast of *The Inheritors*, Peter Egan and Bill Maynard, both said, with tongue in cheek, that I should not forget them if ever I wanted to cast a couple of good actors – they were the two I should remember! All my friends and colleagues congratulated me and when I asked my managers why I had been chosen out of so many good staff members on the short list, the answer I was given surprised me.

"You have travelled around and have a wide experience in theatre and television. You have ideas and all that came down in your favour."

Lord Harlech's vision was for a dynamic company made up of young, dedicated and enthusiastic people. He wanted the young to be pushing the company forward. I was 33 and had made it, I reckoned, by the skin of my teeth.

CHAPTER 14

"Don't Click your Fingers at me Young Man"

PETER ELIAS JONES was the head of children's programmes in HTV Wales in the early 1970s and I was to be placed under his supervision as a first-year trainee programme director. Peter's rise to such a prominent position was perfectly understandable. He was bright, intelligent, creative, smart with people and smart in dress. He spoke fluent Welsh, played the violin, and came from Llangefni, on Anglesey. He was educated there and went on to achieve a joint honours in English and Music at the University of Leeds. Under Aled Vaughan, the controller of programmes for HTV Wales, Peter had prospered. He was a floor manager for a short while before becoming the company's youngest programme director on daily news programmes. His achievements when I joined his department in 1973 were the growing number of Welsh children's programmes for which he was responsible. *Miri Mawr* (Lots of Fun) was a strange programme set in a cave with an odd assortment of subterranean, comic, cartoon creatures, totally unidentifiable, but who all spoke Welsh and caused mischief and havoc. The plots were simply laid out and in each programme – there were three in a week – a presenter would emerge, tumbling down a chute into the cave and become entangled in the lives of the cave's inhabitants. Three *Miri Mawr*s were recorded on a Thursday and three other programmes with an educational slant were recorded on a Friday. Add to this, various quiz programmes, making Peter's department a formidable one in terms of programme output. The department only had a small staff, two researchers, two production assistants and an associated producer. Peter carried overall responsibility, and it was into this power house of mayhem that I found myself training to become a fully fledged programme director. I had one shortcoming, however, and that was my lack of conversational Welsh, although I had a basic understanding of the language. Everything took me twice as long and preparation for my first programme took an immense amount of time and work.

In some ways, the discipline imposed on me in those days stayed with me for the rest of my career. I always prepared thoroughly and never left things to chance. Not only did I have to struggle understanding the language and receive verbal translations, but the programmes needed to be conceptualized for the screen, planned and plotted with all the meetings and administration involved. Prop lists, make-up and wardrobe lists, camera scripts for cast and crew, shot cards for cameramen, meetings with the senior members of the crew to iron out problems and to explain what I was aiming to do. Floor plans of the studio had to be marked up, illustrating cameras and boom and their positions on the floor. Where were artistes standing? Where were they moving to? The lighting department had to know.

Working out the sequence of shots and the sound on a studio camera script would take me an age in those early days. If the script was written to fill 20 minutes, I would take hours to add my camera shots and work out moves for cameras and artistes. My visual sense was being sharpened up – seeing everything through a 3 x 4 shape – which was the basic ratio of a television picture in those days. I had to learn to compose camera shots in my mind and translate them to paper.

On my first day in the gallery I was agitated but tried to stay relaxed. My past experience in the Grampian gallery helped. I became so wound up in the opening sequence of the programme, I ignored the coffee break and the crew became agitated, as well. I had planned a complicated 'James Bond' opening sequence with our presenter playing the secret agent shooting at the camera and the picture turning blood red. A clever idea, but technically too complicated for the amount of work we had facing us. Peter guided me where possible, sat with me much of the time and helped unravel my complicated camera script and asked, with a grin on his face, whether we were doing *Ben Hur*. On another occasion he would say, "Look luv – if in doubt, lock off on a wide shot and break for coffee."

Peter and I developed a good working relationship; he could lose his temper and we would often cross swords but the amount of laughter and good, solid advice I received from him always outweighed those moments of misery. The crews were wonderful, provided you respected them and sought their advice. There were troublemakers who protected their own corner, and those who worked to every union rule – possibly those who had survived the TWW and HTV franchise change. Generally though, there were some very talented and highly skilled technicians and it is to them I would turn if I encountered a challenge. The presenter one week was supposed to be an inventor who could make himself invisible – I had a feeling the writers would throw that one at me! Working out how to make him slowly disappear and reappear produced endless discussions with the technicians, but the effect looked quite stunning. Flashing lights and tilted shots for pop groups and mechanical devices to fix to the camera to create multiple images were all part of my learning curve. If *Top of the Pops* could do it, then why not *Miri Mawr*, which I understood later was becoming cult viewing with the students of the university in Bangor.

Audrey was the senior vision mixer and had worked for TWW. I did not have to hit the buttons with sweaty palms like those days in Grampian. She was there, employed as a vision mixer, and very good she was too. Audrey called a spade a spade and if anything upset her, she was quick to mention it.

I developed the nasty habit of clicking my fingers every time I wanted to cut from one camera to the other. She stopped rehearsal.

"Don't you click your fingers at me young man!" she would say with annoyance in her voice and her brows furrowed. Audrey had saved the skin of many directors and had taken the right shot at the right time, especially on live news.

"Look love," she said to me afterwards. Audrey knew how to keep cool and working that desk was mastery in itself, but she had a short fuse if you annoyed her and she possibly had trainee directors for breakfast. "If you dream up something complicated in the programme, please call me at home any time day or night so we can discuss it. I will think it through and work out how it can be done on the mixer. If you ask me to take Camera 1 and superimpose Camera 2 and then add Camera 3 on a caption and then wipe across to a film, we have a problem, but we might be able to solve it with discussion and planning. Call me first, OK love?"

It was good advice and taught me the lesson that television programmes were brought together by a whole team of people who needed to be led and directed, but also demanded to be consulted if anything out of the ordinary was to happen. It was team effort. Most importantly it was a time to learn how to make decisions. Making decisions and making it known that I was the decision-maker was a big hurdle to jump when confronted by some people who thought they knew better. Only one person 'carried the can' and that was the producer, and I was right up there next to him. From there on in, I held planning meetings for every studio programme I directed, to which all heads of departments were invited and expected to attend.

Nadia was part of the programme planning department who allocated the time slots for our programmes. If my programme was meant to run for 25 minutes and 30 seconds, then that was final. Nadia's day was split into hours, minutes and seconds and no director was allowed to overrun his time without

169

permission from Nadia. Every commercial break, every news bulletin, every film and every programme, whether it was local or national, was timed in advance and the daily and nightly transmission plan was sacrosanct, with Nadia standing guard. A telephone conversation with Nadia would go like this:

"Good morning, Nadia. I would appreciate an extra 30 seconds for my programme…"

"NO, DAVID."

"Please Nadia, only 30 seconds."

"I cannot afford you another five seconds David; we are running in to a live *Coronation Street* at the end of your programme, so I cannot conjure up seconds out of nowhere."

"Please, please Nadia."

Nadia was a formidable lady and knew how to put down a programme director. "No," and that was the end of the argument. On another day she would grant me a reprieve:

"David, this is Nadia. Would you like another 20 seconds for your programme next week? Yorkshire Television is running under with *The Bob Monkhouse Show*."

I would offer a silent prayer of thanks to Bob Monkhouse and pay homage to Nadia. One never refused extra time when it was offered.

There is no doubt that my job and the time it took up had a dampening effect on my family life. Talk to my elder daughter today about her dad in those early days, and she will recall the weekends of floor plans, scripts and lists. It was work, work and more work, and not much time for family life.

My training continued for nearly nine months and in that department I was to find myself working on every programme. My two production assistants worked ceaselessly to type out everything I gave them on a Monday morning. There were no computers, just the clatter of typewriters. No programme would see the light of day without a production assistant (PA). They would have everything typed and timed in readiness for Wednesday afternoon rehearsals. Everything had to run to time. They knew how long each programme was in advance;

sometimes they went begging to the programme planning department for extra time and were sometimes lucky enough to get it; other times the answer was a definite 'no' and cuts would have to be made in the scripts or I would have to work the programme faster.

I knew so little of location filming with one camera or what the film editor would require in the way of raw footage to put a sequence together that would make sense to the viewer. The film editor was a creature unknown to me, and Peter Elias Jones must have grown grey hairs trying to make me understand the very basics of filming and film editing. "Think cutting room," he would say. "Think cutting room. Think how your shots are going to be put together in the cutting room."

My very first day of directing a film crew: two presenter-actors sliding a boat down a bank onto the lake near the Port Talbot steelworks was without inspiration and imagination. I could not see how a sequence could be put together using just one camera. I produced shots with nothing happening within the frame. The cameraman was not interested. I was failing to fire anyone's imagination. Filming a sequence of Father Christmas arriving was another disaster. "Think cutting room, David. Think cutting room." The words would not penetrate. I had the film editors shouting for something decent to cut and Peter called me back from holiday to cast my eye over the useless footage I had shot up in Colwyn Bay Mountain Zoo. The sequences did not cut together and I had virtually allowed the cameraman to shoot what he wanted. The trouble is the cameraman does not attend the cutting room, nor does he have to. What was going on? My creative eye had disappeared between the studio and the great outdoors, and I was struggling yet again to make sense of it all. Over the course of time, however, something must have clicked and a whole new set of skills fell into place, but not without the help of people like Peter and some outstanding technicians. My films might not have equalled those of Steven Spielberg's but they passed the quality test.

Filming a sequence on Aberystwyth promenade involved one of the characters from *Miri Mawr* walking the prom, eating an ice cream and slipping on a banana skin – this took an afternoon to achieve. I did it in 25 camera shots and asked for the camera motor to be cranked up to achieve a slow-motion effect on the ice cream sailing up into the air and coming down to the pavement with a splat. It cut together well in the cutting room with some comic music added to the sound track, despite the cost of numerous ice creams to get the shot I wanted. To achieve another effect, this time from a Welsh legend – of the devil himself jumping out of a church tower and landing on a gravestone – I arranged for the cameraman to throw his camera out of the tower. We attached a rope to the camera and wrapped it in blankets with the lens protruding, started the film running and threw it out over the parapet as Peter Elias Jones arrived and nearly collapsed in horror at the sight. He had visions of the cost of a broken 16mm Arriflex camera on his desk. The sequence worked and Peter recalled the story many years later with great amusement.

I had completed seven months of training when Peter allowed my name to go out on the screen for the first time. I rang my Mum and Dad to give them the news. During the bad old days when I struggled to find work, they never lost hope for me and were always on hand to listen and offer guidance and money, no matter how tight my situation. They sat and watched *Miri Mawr* one Thursday afternoon and glowed with pride as my name appeared on the screen. My Dad died of a heart attack a fortnight later. He was 67.

***

I had finished training and the internal phone rang.

"David, I've checked with Peter. Could you help me out next week please and direct the news?"

The order came from Anne, the programme controller's secretary. The whole week ahead was torture as I mentally tried to delay the inevitable. I sat in with the news director every night watching the Welsh and English news being directed from the gallery. Dear God, it was fast and it was live. I had never done a live programme before and to make matters worse, the script for both programmes was not readily available until 20 minutes to six, sometimes later: transmission was at 6 p.m. Those next 20 minutes were frantic. The stories were put in order by the news editor and the director would break the script down and allocate the visuals accompanying the stories to various film and slide machines. Studio cameras were given their tasks; there were presenters and live interviews to cover in the studio, but with no rehearsal time – just a call-out from the gallery with the PA counting me down to transmission. There were approximately a crew of 25 people awaiting direction. What I couldn't understand was how so much could be covered by only three cameras, and then my mind switched to Anglia and Grampian and the way Hector would cover six talking heads in the studio by using three cameras to their maximum. *Y Dydd* and *Report Wales*, split by a commercial break was, in my humble opinion, a disaster waiting to happen and as sure as eggs are eggs, I would be at the helm when it happened.

The day of transmission arrived and had it not been for well-seasoned production assistants who knew the news routine inside out, I would have stumbled seriously, which is why I always had every respect for a good PA. The experience, however, had a huge element of risk, but an overwhelming feeling of satisfaction if things went well. I came to the conclusion that live news was like Russian roulette. You pulled the trigger and hoped for the best!

My time in the children's department concluded after five years. It had consolidated many of the elements of television programme directing. I had directed everything, from choirs and orchestras to ventriloquists and scientific experiments. I had learned much and worked hard and, at the end, I was directing everything Peter was putting my way. Annette and

I bought a house in Cardiff, closer to my place of work. The controller of programmes asked me whether I would like to do news and current affairs for the next six months and, to be honest with you dear reader, despite the trepidation associated with live programmes, that didn't seem such a bad idea. I needed the experience and possibly the adrenalin that every live news programme generated.

CHAPTER 15

The Home Team

IF YOU WALK through Llandaff fields in Cardiff today and wander down to the housing estate that is situated between Pontcanna and busy Western Avenue, you would be forgiven for hearing from an open window on a hot day the ghostly, echoing din of the old HTV Wales newsroom: frantic, frenetic, fast and furious. The room is smoke-filled and newspaper-strewn, the clatter of typewriters can be heard, the clunking of feet running up and down the stairs, voices shouting durations of links and lead-ins, there are nicotine-stained fingers, blue with carbon paper, hammering the keys and clicking the stop watches. And suddenly the cacophony of noise is silenced by the 'shout'. Stuart's shout. Stuart Leyshon, our beloved news editor is shouting the order of stories for that evening's news programme and anyone missing that shout would die a death during transmission. The journalists are sharp and incisive in their writing – not a second more nor a second less – and the only sound to be heard above Stuart's voice is the whirring Steenbeck film-editing machines in the rooms down the corridor. Film coming up wet from the processing bath, being cut and joined together by editors with one eye on the spools of celluloid and the other on the clock.

In the 1970s, work in the newsroom taught me many things. One was speed. To think at speed, to decide at speed and to act decisively. It also taught me to take more notice of newspapers, to scan the stories and to watch journalists write for television with all the economy and style that made them great at their job. I was there, not to write, but put their words, phrases and pictures through the mechanisms of television. And there was fun... such great fun when life was more relaxed in the club after the show or at morning meetings with the head of news, film crews awaiting their orders from Cardiff to Bangor, reporters scribbling on their pads, with me, planning how I was going to use the studio and all the facilities at my disposal that night. If I learned the knack of staying cool in a crisis, it all came from my years on news. And then there were the characters and those funny moments. There was always laughter in the newsroom.

Martyn Lewis of ITN once asked Mike Lloyd-Williams, our leading presenter/reporter, why he did not go and work in London? Mike replied, "You might be a big cheese in London but I walk tall in Penygraig."

Mike, when interviewing Richard Burton on the train from Paddington to Port Talbot, said to the great film star after the interview, "All I have to offer you, is a packet of Woodbines and a small bottle of scrumpy bought from a shop in Tonypandy this morning," to which the great man replied in the voice that had wooed millions, "Bloody marvellous – take me there, take me there."

If things went wrong on transmission, one did one's best to salvage the mess. I will never forget Alan Rustad sitting in a nice easy chair and beside him was a table lamp on a coffee table. He talked to camera and made a gesture, knocking the lamp off the table. The pieces scattered everywhere. When I cut to the weatherman at the weather map, a little chap on his hands and knees crawled into the shot with a pan and brush to clear the fragments. My voice rose two octaves and I'm sure I was heard in Barry!

A colleague once told of the set collapsing during a live studio discussion. Nothing could be done other than continue the discussion amongst the debris. Two major things could go wrong on news in those days. The films could be in the wrong order on the spool on the machine upstairs. Secondly, the filmed items might fail to arrive. News items from north Wales had to be driven down to Cardiff by van every day. News was not allowed to happen in Bangor after midday! In summer, the driver would complete the journey in record time. In winter, with snow and ice on the Horseshoe Pass, the situation became critical. Many a time we would sit in the gallery with ten minutes to go, and the internal phone would ring and someone would say, "north Wales film has just arrived and it's gone into processing." We would move the item further down the running order to facilitate the processing and late edit. Changing the running order was a devilish job in those early days but we somehow managed it. I suppose we were the primitive pioneers.

The other vital development, of course, in the world of television technology, has been the advent of the digital electronic news camera which does away with film and the laborious business of processing it in a tank of chemicals. The unions fought its introduction but, inwardly, we all knew it made common sense to move with the times. However, in my early newsroom days the mistakes or 'cock-ups' were inevitable. Once, the newsreader read a story about some enormous Christmas pudding and up came shots of the Queen Mother. There was also the story about nuns in west Wales and the sound effects played over the film were tractor engines revving up. There was always a post-mortem the following morning when it was discovered that communications had failed somewhere along the line.

My two worst moments on evening news came on two different nights. I went on air with absolutely nothing in the gate, meaning that no filmed stories had arrived: I had two presenters in the studio and all their stories were what we called 'lead-ins' to film. The monitors in the gallery showed me the output from each of four film projectors which were as bare as Mother Hubbard's cupboard. The editor in charge rang the cutting room upstairs and we were told the film was on its way. Maybe he should have asked whether it was to be 'on its way' today or tomorrow. With three minutes to go, I remained cool. I had known tighter moments on transmission. The PA announced there were now two minutes to go before transmission. I had worked out that the opening sequence to the programme, which I did have, was approximately 20/25 seconds. If the film arrived with a minute to go, there would still be time for the technicians to lace it up and I would see a figure 'six' in the gate – a six second run-up. The PA announced one minute to go. No film. The editor rang the newsroom and yelled at someone to go and check what the 'hell' was going on in the cutting room. "Thirty seconds," called the PA. The presenters could hear my voice in their ear-pieces.

"If the film does not arrive, go to your spare stories and take your time reading. I will tell you when I have the first film in the gate. Everything's fine. I will keep you posted."

Presenters like to be reassured if things are going wrong. The vision mixer asked me what I was going to do. I had no plan.

"Thirty seconds to air" announced the PA. I told her we would continue as if the film was there. I quickly made contact with master control, the people who send the programmes out to the Welsh transmitters, to make them aware of the situation. We then learned the presenters had no spare stories to read. The editor in the corner phoned the newsroom to instruct that every spare story was brought down to the studio as quickly as possible.

"Hello master control. This is David in studio 2. We might have to abort the programme, I will keep you in touch."

"On air in 15 seconds," shouted the PA. No film and no spare stories.

"Thank you, David, we will be standing by." They would fill transmission time with cartoons or something similar if the studio failed to deliver.

"I feel sick," said the vision mixer.

"You'll be fine, follow me," I reassured her.

What a bloody mess, I think to myself. The PA interrupts my thoughts.

"Fifteen seconds studio... on air in 10..." Still no film! "9..." Still no film! "8..." Still no film! "7..." No film! "6..."

I roll the titles and speak to the presenters; they are in the firing line. I tell Tweli Griffiths to read his lead-in and I will then ring his desk phone. The PA again.

"Coming out of titles in 5, 4, 3, 2, 1."

I take Tweli on Camera 2. He reads his lead-in and I ring his phone. He picks it up.

"Hand across to Russell," the news editor and I shout simultaneously.

Tweli apologises to camera and hands over to Russell. Russell reads his lead-in and hands back to Tweli. Russell then leans back in his chair and puts his feet on the desk. He does not want me coming back to him. Thanks Russell. That's great! Spare stories have been thrust around the heavy studio door. I ask Tweli to read all the spares, but slowly. The news editor now has a blood-red complexion. Eight minutes into the start of the programme, the film arrives in the gate but there is not sufficient programme time left to play all the films. *Y Dydd* that night looked rough. There were two weeks to go before the programme finished completely and the new S4C started up. Tweli reminded viewers of this fact and said maybe we should have finished tonight after such a fiasco. No time to dwell on the incident. We are on the commercial break, a new PA has arrived in the gallery and all the films are there.

"Spool through the *Y Dydd* films, to the *Report Wales* films," I instruct the lads upstairs manning the telecine machines.

The Welsh presenters, looking none the worse for wear, change places with the English presenters.

The PA speaks. "Coming to *Report Wales* in 10... 9... etc., etc."

The post-mortem the following morning reveals that the holiday replacement film editor had held on to the Welsh films until he had finished cutting the English ones. (What a dickhead, I think to myself.)

The second major incident happened some years later. Again no tapes had arrived. Tapes had now replaced film. The only two items I had were of a weatherman standing at his weather map and a tape of a man in Carmarthen who manufactured meat pasties. With a minute to go I yelled down the phone to the newsroom and I rarely yelled.

"THERE IS LESS THAN A MINUTE TO GO AND ALL I HAVE DOWN HERE IS A WEATHERMAN AND A BLOODY PASTY. GET MOVING!"

The 'tease', previewing the content of the programme at the top of the show, was one critical area that divided the men from the boys, or the women from the girls. It was not uncommon to have fragments of the programme split between six different sources with fast 'voice-overs' in between. Get that wrong and it sat with you for the remainder of the programme. Get it right and you were in with a chance. Trainee directors and PAs would go pale at the thought of doing it and one lady, I remember, declared enough was enough and sped speedily out of the newsroom...

***

Moving between news and current affairs was a common occurrence. Current affairs usually involved studio work and a great deal of outside filming in all weathers. There was the Royal Welsh Show every year at Llanelwedd; a hard week on the feet, but a wonderful week if the weather was fine. I worked the Royal Welsh for eight years with Mike Lloyd-Williams, until I fell off a bale of hay and broke a bone in my wrist. I worked on programmes covering a wide range of topics from political and cultural to industrial, educational and farming. I travelled the length and breadth of Wales, and very often ended up in London, in the Welsh Office or on the terraces of the House of Commons. There was coverage of all the major

Welsh industries ranging from steel making in Llanwern, Port Talbot and Shotton, tin and motorcar radiators in Llanelli, to Christmas decorations and toy manufacture in Merthyr. We filmed at Hotpoint and Hoover, Sharp electronics in north Wales, Sony and Panasonic in the south. There was extensive coverage of strikes and industrial unrest in the 1970s and 1980s, the miners' strike and the break-up of communities. There were programmes on the motorcar and the motor component industry, and also on the technological advances in Wales. Whatever was happening in our nation, HTV covered it and provided that all-important local service keeping our viewers informed. Such was the popularity of the channel, the story went round that during a period of financial difficulty in the company, a whip-round was conducted in one of the valley pubs! Often if MPs could not make it to our Cardiff studio, we went to London and hired independent television studios in Soho. *Yr Wythnos* was often transmitted live to Wales on a Monday night, a stone's throw from striptease parlours and clip joints.

***

I went to America with Mike Lloyd-Williams and a crew to cover the Johnny Owen story – the Merthyr boxer they called the 'matchstick man'. In 1980 he had gone to the Olympic Auditorium in Los Angeles to fight Lupe Pintor for the WBC bantamweight title. Johnny was knocked down twice in round twelve and remained unconscious following the second knockdown and was rushed to hospital to remove a blood clot from his brain. He died two months later. We met the family who were at his bedside and filmed at the gymnasium and at the auditorium where the fight took place. We also covered the funeral in Merthyr Tydfil; the whole town turned out to give Johnny a hero's farewell.

***

It is now with hindsight I look back and realise how close I was to the very fabric of Welsh life. The newsroom and the current affairs department explored and reflected every aspect of political, economic, industrial and cultural change. We covered crime, storm and tempest, droughts, kidnaps, oil spills, accidents and tragedies. There were stories about bishops, vicars and explorers, historians and men and women of courage. With my friends and colleagues, many of whom were journalists and technicians, we covered the building of the M4 into south Wales, and the development of the A55 to Holyhead. There was the closure of pits and all the old Welsh industries, union disputes, the modernising of old landscapes. There were always interviews with MPs and major decision makers: Gwynfor Evans winning Carmarthen for Plaid Cymru and later threatening his fast to death for a Welsh fourth channel. We looked at jobs and unemployment, factory closures, the work of the Welsh quangos and the planning and declaring of the new Welsh Assembly.

We covered all the general and local elections. My first experience of working an outside broadcast, a studio gallery on wheels but more cramped, was covering the first Welsh devolution referendum in 1979 which resulted in a 'no' vote. Many other OBs were to follow including Labour's shock defeat in 1992 when we were covering Islwyn, Neil Kinnock's constituency.

When Jim Callaghan was nearing the end of his political life in 1979, we covered his movements during the election count back at his Cardiff constituency, this time as Prime Minister. ITN had commissioned us to cover the count and Callaghan's flat where it was hoped we would get an interview. No one was totally sure, however, whether he would be at the flat or in a local hotel. Word on the grapevine was that he was going to the hotel, and I informed ITN accordingly. The grapevine was right. Mr Callaghan was at the hotel. We would catch him as he was coming out and grab an interview. Unfortunately it looked as if he was going to follow the count from his bedroom television and then retire in the early hours. At 2 a.m., after communicating with ITN, I stood the crew down and we all went into the hotel for a warming cup of tea. Half an hour later my walkie-talkie lit up and a colleague on Callaghan's floor informed me that the Prime Minister and his entourage were leaving the hotel. I yelled like a man possessed, and cups and saucers went flying as 20 technicians rushed out of the hotel and scrambled up the grassy bank to the OB vehicles and started firing them up. Alas, Mr Callaghan was quicker than we were. As pictures became recordable, all we had was a shot of the car's tail-lights disappearing down the M4. The electorate was favouring Mrs Thatcher and Mr Callaghan was returning post-haste to London. This would be the last day of his premiership. He had outwitted us and I felt responsible.

Among the triumphs there were many disappointments. Unfortunately, we were victims of considerable over-manning in those days and totally inflexible in our working practice. Today, a reporter with a small, digital camera would have captured the moment; whether Mr Callaghan would have given the interview, with his fate so close, seems quite unlikely.

And then there was Richard Burton's funeral – I think he had about three – but the Pontrhydyfen one was the one that returned me to my childhood holidays with my grandmother, walking the viaducts and sliding down the coal tips eating cold chips from a paper bag. The journalist with me on this occasion was Ron Lewis, also from Aberystwyth, whom I had met for the first time in the newsroom. Ron reminded me who his father was: the great Walter Lewis, who had influenced me so much to continue being a local magician in my early teens. Ron tells the story of a programme director in the newsroom being told by an editor that he was just a button pusher. The director responded immediately, "I am not a button pusher, I merely tell other people what buttons to push."

I travelled to Ireland twice and tasted the Guinness more than once. It's true the black, creamy stuff does not travel well and is best consumed in Ireland! Two trips to Israel followed, one at Christmas, where soldiers with machine guns stood near the Christmas trees in Manger Square. The other trip was for an interview with a pro-Palestinian priest from Machynlleth. Our guide, who worked for the Government, wanted to hear the interview. I refused her permission to be at the interview. We filmed two interviews, one for her and the other for transmission. That night our van was searched but Jack, our sound technician, slept with the tapes under his pillow.

On another occasion, we were in Brussels filming Welsh farmers making demands for money towards snow damage to their land and crops. The crew and I were in a lift in the EU building when the lift decided to stop between floors and all the lights went out. Nothing could be more frightening. Suddenly from the blackness in the lift, a transvestite with blonde hair emerged into a shaft of daylight and started yelling in French into the intercom demanding an immediate release from her predicament. On came the lights, down went the lift and up went my lifelong distrust of elevator cars.

All of this was for a Welsh current affairs programme on S4C. HTV Wales had put in a bid for doing the news in Welsh on this new channel. At some expense we piloted two news programmes using the ITN studio in London – my one and only time to direct from the ITN gallery – and it was awesome. However, the politics of editorial control intervened. HTV Wales was to finally produce current affairs for S4C and the BBC in Cardiff would look after their Welsh news.

It was then off to Japan, guests of Sharp Electronics who had brought good fortune to Deeside in north Wales. In Germany, we were scrutinized by soldiers with binoculars standing on their vantage point sentry boxes studying our movements around the Berlin wall. In Communist-held East Berlin, we all felt the gloom of that regime. It was freezing cold and soldiers hid their faces whenever they saw our camera. I will never forget the snow-covered graves by that hideous wall – in memory of the fallen who had craved Western freedom and jumped this grey, ugly, man-made blockade.

We flew to Zimbabwe where we met many Welsh people, families living under the Mugabe dictatorship in beautiful houses surrounded with twelve foot high walls and padlocks on the gates. This trip was fondly remembered for being able to sit in a light aircraft over the Victoria Falls – what a wonderful, breathtaking sight.

And then my final trip to America with Professor Garyl Rees, to Pittsburgh, the location of the headquarters of Alcoa Steel which had a base in Wales, and also the enormous 3M company which had a base in Gorseinon and manufactured everything from video tape to Sellotape. We met and interviewed the man who invented the 'Post-it' note for the 3M company – a certain Mr Art Fry. Here was a man who knew his glues and pastes and every conceivable type of adhesive.

The 1979 ITV strike was one of the longest, costliest and the most bitter – all of it because of pay scales, the introduction of electronic cameras, and editing. During my career with ITV there had been many strikes and walk-outs. Many of them were called in the afternoon, which put a great strain on those of us working towards a six o'clock deadline. The strike was national and went on for ten weeks; staff started looking for jobs elsewhere. Some went and worked on the building of the new M4 motorway, others in shops and driving taxis. One of our production assistants started selling bridal wear in a Cardiff shop. Stories abounded. A member of staff at ATV in Birmingham took a waiter's job in a very smart restaurant. One lunchtime he found himself waiting at table and serving the executives of his own company. Leading up to the strike, employees from each ITV company had their own sad story to tell as to why they had been locked out. With us, it was due to the problem of management setting up the lighting rigs instead of our qualified electricians. This action resulted in ACTT members refusing to work in a 'potentially unsafe studio'. I always felt like the Judas on these occasions, as did a great many of us. I could see the value of belonging to the union, my salary bore witness to that, but I always preferred negotiation to a lock-out. Feelings ran high and work was interrupted. As for the viewers around the whole of the UK, they went without their ITV service. Annette and I now had two children, Naomi being the second baby nine years later. I seem to remember us getting free milk for her because I was on strike.

I recall one other incident involving the union that was to affect me personally. On a film documentary in north Wales, a technician started to sabotage the shoot and land me and other technicians in hot water. I reported the incident and management took action and threatened him with dismissal. Three members of the union brotherhood approached me and they were not happy people. I was instructed to act with leniency and convince management that he was doing a good job. The occasion, however, did not arise, and our troubled technician resigned and joined the BBC. Once again he started to make trouble and the Corporation, with some justification, asked him to leave. Was it a good union? Yes it was, but the delicate balance between union membership and loyalty to the company was a sensitive issue that I had hoped to avoid at all costs.

***

Pope John Paul II visited Wales in June 1982 and held a Mass before an enormous crowd at Pontcanna Fields, in close proximity to our studio. Bob Symonds, our head of news, and I were locked into a hot, stuffy, little technical area recording highlights for the evening's programme. There were no windows, so we were denied the chance of actually seeing the Pope in the flesh. Bob was working for that night's news while I was gathering highlights for John Mead, one of our senior producers. John called the highlights, 'golden moments', and was constantly calling me on the talk-back system that connected him in the studio to me in my hot box upstairs.

"David Lloyd – there's another golden moment."

If I heard that shout for 'golden moments' one more time, I would scream. The Pontiff kissed a child on the head.

"ANOTHER GOLDEN MOMENT, DAVID LLOYD."

I screamed!

Bob and I never did get to see the Pope in the flesh and Bob only saw him when he went on holiday to Italy later that year.

I worked on news and current affairs for ten years and loved every moment. It was a nail-biting experience that left me breathless but with a taste for live news and current affairs for the rest of my natural life. Charlie Smith up in Grampian had been right all those years ago, telling me to go and work in the newsroom if I wanted drama. In return for all the experience I had gained in the newsroom, I gave them reliability and dependability; there was a continuity in having a permanent director attached to the place and a production staff who were committed to the successful transmission of daily news bulletins. I had begun to see how the blending of good research, leading to sharp informative writing, could work so effectively with good pictures and sound. Sometimes marketed as the 'home team', our journalists were the best in the business and the stories they uncovered were passionately told. There was an integrity and balance. It was a solid and dependable service, informative and popular with viewers. Above all the attributes, it was an admired news service reflecting a changing Wales and nothing made it more important than that.

CHAPTER 16

The Sun Will Come Out Tomorrow

IF EVER THERE was a nudge towards developing and producing my own programmes, then *Tomorrow's Star Maybe* could be defined as the catalyst.

Sitting in the newsroom one day, I read about little Suzie Kemeys, a schoolgirl from Cwmbrân who had been chosen to play the part of little orphan Annie in the musical, *Annie*, at London's Victoria Palace theatre. I shared the story with Alan Rustad. He too had read the same article and simultaneously we both thought it would make a cracking story for a filmed documentary at a time when most of the stories coming out of the newsroom could be classified as hard news. Here was a tale of a little girl from south Wales who came from a working-class background and was going to find herself under the spotlight on a West End stage. It was the stuff that fairy stories are made of. Alan could see the words and I could see the pictures, it was a perfect combination of both. We had worked together in the past, not only on the daily news but up in north Wales on a behind-the-scenes look at the Llangollen Eisteddfod. Alan did a spot of research and made a few phone calls to Suzie's home, and I rang the theatre to arrange a visit to one of the performances. It also seemed a good idea to chat with our contracts department regarding the use of schoolgirls in our programme. Armed with sufficient information we approached our head of news and spelt out the plan. He was not opposed to the idea, gave us the go-ahead and said it would fit the Friday night's *Outlook* slot which was 25 minutes 30 seconds. For my part, I felt this was a break-a-way from the newsroom. It was an opportunity to direct and co-produce something with Alan, whom I regarded as a very smooth operator and a highly intelligent journalist.

The research was fruitful. Suzie was one of a clutch of girls who played the part of Annie. Being underage, the rules and regulations governing the use of children on the professional stage or film are there for their own protection. Suzie gave about two or three performances a week, the rest of the time she was being tutored in her school lessons and being chaperoned around London and between the theatre and a flat with other children from the show. As the show is centred around a New York orphanage, there were plenty of other kids playing the part of orphans. We drew up plans and went up to see the show in London one afternoon. It soon became apparent that the programme would need some extracts from the stage show itself.

We would start shooting in Suzie's home and interview her mother. She would tell us how Suzie had been spotted in a talent show at a holiday camp. We would then shoot some sequences of Suzie herself at school, in the classroom with the other pupils, and walking out of school with all her friends. Final sequences would be shot in London, backstage at the Victoria Palace preparing for the show, and the girls taking their place before the curtain went up at the beginning of the show.

We planned filming in the flat where the girls stayed, interviews with the chaperone, Suzie's friends, and the producer of *Annie*. We then planned the expensive bit, shooting three or four sequences on the stage with Suzie, the other girls, and the orchestra. We would film Suzie on the set singing, 'Tomorrow (The Sun Will Come Out)', a song full of hope for the little girls from the orphanage, and 'It's a Hard Knock Life' – a song

189

sung by all the little orphans as they 'bang' away on the floor with their cleaning buckets and brushes. There would also be vox pops with members of the audience who would come streaming out of the theatre at the end of the show. At this point Alan made the discovery that Suzie was not the only Welsh girl in the show; there were two others. Helen Thorne, came from Penarth, and had already done her stint playing the lead role. The third girl was from Swansea, Catherine Zeta Jones – a name at the time that was not particularly memorable. Catherine was about twelve years of age and, like the other girls, still in school. I wish now, with hindsight, we had interviewed Catherine; it would have made interesting footage for those later years. We did however film the three of them in the flat and on the stage.

The orchestra were all on Musicians Union rates, as were the backstage staff, and I was taking a Cardiff crew up to London with hotel expenses and overnight allowances. The head of news was not a happy man when he saw the cost of the operation. This was no half-hour news programme. Alan and I persuaded him to think otherwise; it was a family tale with lovely music and a girl from Cwmbrân in the lead role. What more would the viewers want late on a Friday night after coming out of the pub and settling themselves down in an easy chair in front of the telly? I negotiated for a full hour-long documentary to justify the cost and somehow managed to get the budget but there was to be no overtime allowed. That final point was repeatedly stressed.

With everything taken into account, this was a big programme for the newsroom and was the butt of many jokes for weeks to come. For me it was an important milestone. I was co-producing it with Alan and inwardly I knew it was the launch pad for so much more.

The components of the programme were filmed over a fortnight with Alan and I having to work other programmes in addition to the documentary. The musical items had to be done in one afternoon with the girls, with other members of the cast and all the musicians present. It took us all morning to complete the sound rig, wiring our sound system into the theatre's system. Orchestra and cast were at the ready and the whole afternoon was sheer joy. Finally, we had Alan's opening link to do which was 30 seconds long – his opening piece to camera which I would like him to do on the orphanage set. The front-of-house curtain would rise and on would come Alan to deliver his link to the camera in the balcony. The orchestra and cast left the theatre. It was 4.45 p.m. and we had to be finished by 5 p.m.. otherwise the theatre crew would be on golden time and I would never be trusted with another programme.

"Camera ready?" I asked.

"Yes, sir," came Robin's reply.

"Sound," I shouted.

"All set," said Jack from the wings.

"Steve ready with the tabs?" (curtains)

"Yes," shouted Steve from backstage.

"Stand by, Alan," I shouted down to Alan.

"Ready to go, Dave," he called back.

"Turn over camera, turn over sound," I instructed.

"Turning over and stable," shouted Jack.

"Turning over," replied the muffled voice of Robin Higginson, with his eye looking into the camera.

I shouted "Action" and the tabs opened and Alan appeared from the wings.

"Stop there. Out of tape," yelled Jack's voice.

"I don't believe it, Jack. Have you got a fresh tape?" I shouted across from the balcony.

"There's one in the car outside, I'll get it now," Jack replied. I looked at my watch. Cenwyn Edwards, our executive producer, looked at his watch. We were all looking at our watches. There was five minutes to go. If Jack did not move and get loaded up with a fresh quarter-inch tape for his tape recorder, we were in the 'proverbial' and David Lloyd would be back doing the nightly news.

Jack moved across the stage at a snail's pace, went out

through the stage door, found a fresh tape in the company Volvo and strolled back in. Meanwhile Alan, standing in the wings, overheard the scene crew saying, "We will soon be in golden time, lads." Jack loaded up and I was having kittens.

"Sound ready," shouted Jack.

"Camera standing by," shouted Robin.

"Turn over camera, turn over sound."

Everyone was ready, there was a minute of working time left and I was beginning to sweat. The palms of my hands were soaked.

"ACTION," I shouted.

The tabs opened, Alan appeared from the wings, looked up to camera, delivered his opening link in the coolest of ways, set the story of this little girl from Cwmbrân who passed the audition and won a place in a top West End show.

"Cut," I shouted. "Check the gate," I yelled.

"Gate clear," shouted the assistant cameraman.

I yelled four words. "WRAP, IT'S A WRAP!"

I looked at my watch, there were ten seconds left to go before golden time, but there was no golden time. We finished ten seconds to 5 p.m., or did we?

"No need to worry, Dave," said Cenwyn, with a smile. "I altered the clocks on the wall backstage. They still think its 4.55!"

Well I'll be jiggered! Executive producers have their uses after all!

When I thanked all the crew and bought them a drink in the pub opposite, I approached Jack and thanked him for getting that tape on time, but told him that I was slightly worried when I saw his snail's pace crossing the stage to go outside to get a fresh tape. Jack, lugubrious, slow-moving, but with a cheeky grin crossing his face said, "Well, Dave. As I saw it, if Uncle Jack had panicked and rushed like a greyhound across that stage, everyone else would have panicked with me, and that would have got us nowhere. Best to take your time see, Dave. No rush. Life is already a battle of wits."

We all laughed. He had a point.

Transmission was a couple of weeks before Christmas. We had about four days to edit and dub whilst working on the news in the evening. Steve did a wonderful job on the edit and Alan's commentary was second to none. I was so pleased with the programme.

I worked on news and current affairs for ten years, but now it was time for pastures new – I wanted to produce my own programmes more than anything else. I had ideas, and one of them I had been researching and developing in my back dining room at home for nearly two years.

CHAPTER 17

Producer/Director

WHEN PROBING AND researching the effects of the Second World War on the home front in Wales, I returned to 1944 when, as a very young child, I would be woken from my slumbers and taken downstairs to my grandmother's kitchen and placed under the table, which was, in reality, a Morrison shelter. It was a cage-like construction and named after Herbert Morrison, the Home Secretary. The first sound of a siren over Cardiff, and the approaching drone of German bombers meant that everyone had to take shelter. I can remember feeling very frightened, but the morning would come and I would go out and look for bits of shrapnel near the bomb sites. HTV Wales gave me the money and the opportunity to relive those memories and make some substantial documentaries on the Welsh home front. It was an awesome project and I had four programmes to make, two in English for HTV Wales and two in Welsh for S4C. We called this back-to-back filming and doubtless the two Welsh programmes would go some way towards subsidising the English programmes. Many excellent programmes on the war had been produced already for television but none had concentrated specifically on Wales. I presented the results of my research to management and was given the go-ahead. It was 1985 and the programmes would celebrate the end of war in Europe in 1945. Much of the research had been done, but I was given two staff researchers to help find interviewees. We advertised in the Welsh press – north and south – for people who had lived through wartime experiences at home. We were inundated with hundreds of letters and each letter had to be followed up.

An expert advised me on the bombing of our cities from a German perspective. The Swansea archivist, Dr John Alban, spoke about the bombing runs on Swansea and the terrible devastation after the three-night Blitz in 1941. Vernon Scott, a journalist from the *Western Telegraph* in Pembroke Dock, was well versed on the bombing of the oil tanks in that town. I called upon the help of university historians in Wales and made contact with two German gentlemen, both ex-Luftwaffe, who had flown on the raids against Swansea, Cardiff and Pembroke Dock namely, pilot Hilmar Schmidt and bomb aimer, Julius Tengler. There were people who could talk about the Americans in Wrexham, the Polish graves in north Wales, the Italian prisoner-of-war camp in Henllan and the camp for high-ranking German officers in Bridgend. We touched on Rudolf Hess being held prisoner in Abergavenny, the storing of the country's valuable works of art in Aberystwyth and north Wales, and Churchill planning and rehearsing D-Day landings on Pembrokeshire beaches. There were sad stories by the score, but also some amusing ones. I liked the one of women painting seam lines down the backs of their bare legs with gravy powder and water to give the impression they were wearing seamed stockings, which was most convincing until it started to rain!

We covered the blackout, the food rationing, the raids on our cities, the munitions' workers, the construction of aircraft, the air-raid shelters and, in Bangor, *It's That man Again (ITMA)*, a weekly radio show with comedian, Tommy Handley. We found a pacifist who refused to fight; and we looked at life before, during and after the war; the dilution of the Welsh culture; the evacuee problem, and the Victory Day street parties. Not a stone was left unturned. My two most expensive items were a helicopter for film shooting over our cities and over what was left of the oil tanks in Pembroke

Dock, and the black and white newsreel footage from the London archives which cost a fortune for television usage. I was charged by the second and needed copyright permission for all of it. I received a call from a gentleman in London who said he had found some film in his attic of a raging fire at some oil tanks. Could I help him identify it? I did more than that, I used it on the programme. It was a blaze at Pembroke Dock, when every fire service from around the country was called there to help quench the flames from oil tanks which had been attacked by a lone German aircraft. The blaze lasted three weeks; five Cardiff firemen were killed in a boiling oil spill and their lives are still remembered on a plaque in Cardiff's Adam Street fire station today. After the programmes were transmitted, I received letters from viewers in Pembrokeshire who, in the archive footage, had recognised their fathers helping to pump water from the sea to the fire fighters at the oil tanks, with the awful realisation that the tide was rapidly receding. The programmes were a tribute to the ordinary Welsh people on the home front, many of whom had lost their lives. Some of those who had survived were happy to speak to me about their experiences during those long years of war.

War Over Wales / Rhyfel Dros Gymru was transmitted in 1985 – four one-hour-long documentaries. They were repeated a year later. There were numerous contributors and 60 production staff, who all helped me pull it together at various stages. Bob Symonds, our news editor in my last few years in the news department, used to look at a successful night's programme and say, "It was a little cracker!" I think the phrase stuck and I'm sure Bob won't mind if I borrow it. At that time, *War Over Wales* really was a little cracker!

***

After the war programmes were completed I went straight into *Does Wales Mean Business?* – six programmes culminating in *The Welsh National Business Awards*. These programmes looked at what was being achieved in Welsh business following the collapse of traditional Welsh industries. The programmes were all about entrepreneurship and encouraging new Welsh business. It was a competition to find the best ideas from bottling fruit on Anglesey to the latest drinking cup for toddlers. The programmes were made in partnership with agencies, banks and newspapers, and the final award ceremony was held in our larger studio in front of a distinguished audience of MPs, leaders of industry, and other men in grey suits. Not the easiest of audiences from which to produce laughter and applause! I would get part of the morning and the whole afternoon to rehearse with five or six cameras, and the programme would be recorded and completed usually one hour before it went out on air which made little allowance for error. Everyone had to be razor sharp and it was sweaty palms and racing hearts all over again. Having tried to relax everyone into believing there was nothing to worry about, I would warm up the audience, perform a few magic tricks, introduce the floor manager and presenters and return to the gallery and lie on the floor and relax and breathe, as per the old Bruford routine. Roz, our vision mixer, would enter the gloom of the gallery, look down and exclaim, "OH MY GOD, DAVID LLOYD'S COLLAPSED." Rose Bruford would have been well pleased.

The pace of work was relentless on the business series and the shooting schedule beyond what could be expected. Editing and transmission loomed closer, which meant three of us, myself, the journalist/presenter and the PA, would race like idiots from one location to another, crisscrossing Wales and even flying up to Glasgow or over to the Isle of Man. Overnight stays in hotels, initially quite exciting, became laborious and tiresome as one plastic bedroom was replaced by another. We would wake in the morning never being absolutely sure where we were. Paul Starling, our presenter and industrial correspondent, would follow me down the A55 in north Wales, both of us travelling at breakneck speed to make the next appointment. "Lloyd," he would say. "In my head, I was writing your obituary. I had the devil's own job to keep up with you."

There was one excruciatingly funny incident when filming two items for *The Welsh National Business Awards* programme. I wanted Paul to deliver a piece to camera from his bed in an award-winning hotel in north Wales. He had no pyjamas in his suitcase and we were miles from home, so he went out and bought some. The following day, the shoot continued on the second item at a small business in Newtown where they made jewellery. Tony, our cameraman, asked whether one of us could go out and buy some women's nylon stockings, the idea being that if you held such fine mesh in front of the camera lens, the jewellery, in close up, really sparkled. Tony's brainwave worked and the close-ups looked very impressive. Somehow the bill for the pyjamas and the nylon stockings ended up on Paul's expense claim and, on his return to the office, the controller called him. "Paul, I have just signed your expenses but I am somewhat puzzled, if not a little worried, about your claim for pyjamas and nylon stockings. Is there something you want to tell me?" Paul and I roared with laughter for months afterwards.

***

Goodbye to business and back outside with two railway documentaries. Only one man had the skill and capability of presenting *See How They Ran* for me, and that was Arfon Haines Davies, a presenter with a solid reputation for professional friendliness, an ex-Aberystwyth boy and a lover of steam trains everywhere. *See How They Ran* was a history of the Cambrian Railway which runs from Shrewsbury to Aberystwyth and Pwllheli, and Dr Stewart Owen Jones was my advisor. I spent a couple of months researching and writing the script and then brought a researcher on board to find the interviewees and get the necessary permissions from British Rail, as it was then. Use of a very expensive helicopter, with the side door removed to accommodate lighting cameraman, Roger Richards, produced some amazing aerial photography of the Cambrian coast. The sequence at the Friog Rocks near Barmouth is breathtakingly wonderful. Arfon would frequently make me laugh by telling the story of when he was a lad in Aberystwyth and his mother would encourage him to go to the Urdd Christmas party. "You must go to the party," she would say. "There will be a tea, Charlie Chaplin and David Lloyd," referring of course to one of my early conjuring shows and the old Charlie Chaplin films. I would feel quite elated by the fact that I had been bracketed along with the great Charlie Chaplin! Arfon said at the time that working on *See How They Ran* and spending time on those summer mornings under the blue skies around the Dovey estuary was an experience that made his work so worthwhile and seem anything but work. For railway historians and steam buffs everywhere, this was a popular programme.

The second railway programme, *Engine Whistle Blowing*, was the story of the little Tal-y-llyn railway that runs on the west Wales coast from Towyn up to Nant Gwernol. Once famous for carrying slate to the roof tops of the world, this lovely little railway had gone into serious decline until rescued in the 1950s by an engineer called L.T.C. Rolt who brought on board a whole collection of enthusiastic railway volunteers – doubtless, the start of railway preservation societies everywhere. This documentary had great conviction and credibility as a result of the presence of our front-of-camera presenter who could be regarded as one of this country's greatest actors, namely Timothy West. He is himself a founder member of the Tal-y-llyn Railway Board. Cenwyn Edwards, my executive producer, had suggested this programme to me and it remains one of my many favourites. I went up to London for lunch and presented Tim with the script. He made the words his own in such a professional way, giving a commentary in the dubbing theatre, and on location, that made one think that he was making up the words as he went along. Both railway programmes were expertly cut on video tape by Simon Johnson, whose understanding of the blend required between music and pictures on a documentary made it look highly professional and a must for everyone to enjoy. This programme was repeated on Channel Four.

I was totally unprepared for the next stage of my career.

CHAPTER 18

Swansong

IT WAS 1988. If one programme drained me of all my human resources, then it had to be the Telethon. Hosted by Michael Aspel in London and presented locally by Arfon Haines Davies and Ruth Madoc, this fund-raising event was originally an American idea, presented by Jerry Lewis. In Cardiff, this 27-hour television marathon was, without question, the biggest beast I had ever worked on in my career. I did not inherit this programme in any gentle way: it was thrust upon me for all manner of reasons. I was the producer of the Welsh section of this country-wide extravaganza and given only three weeks to work on it before transmission.

This overall nationwide event was controlled by LWT in London and, when I met the London producers, there was disbelief that I had been put in charge of the Welsh operation with so little time left before transmission. They gave me enough written rules and regulations governing the broadcast of a telethon to fill a suitcase. I started reading it even before the train left Paddington.

The biggest problem we had was the free advertising that would inevitably happen if we let things get out of control, as there were ITC rules governing the use of advertising on screen. For example, if the staff of some famous high street store were organising an event, like a fund-raising sleep-in or a whacky game in the street outside their shop for the Telethon, they would be perfectly entitled to bandy their name around. If they came into the studio with a big cheque, their name would

201

also be seen on their cheque and on their uniforms – a perfect way of getting free advertising on television, and that kind of commercial saturation was not allowed. Even nightclubs in Cardiff saw it as a way of getting free publicity, inviting stars from *Coronation Street* to the club and our cameras, in turn plugging the club and sending donations to the Telethon. You will have already guessed that this actually happened and I was embroiled in the row between the club's headquarters in London and memos from my managing director. We came out of it clean; I had spelt out the rules to the club manager before we even went near there.

Another major issue was the presenting of the big corporate cheques in London. If Bloggings and Bloggings, who had branches all round the country were presenting a cheque in London, then Bloggings and Bloggings in Cardiff had to present their local Welsh cheque at the same time. Had this rule not applied, Bloggings and Bloggings would have had free saturated advertising all over the country throughout the 27 hours. And yet, the corporate money was important and generously given to good causes in Wales.

We somehow had to minimise the use of the branded name. It could be something like, "Thank you very much, Bloggings and Bloggings. And the amount you have collected is £330. How did you go about raising that money? Wonderful, thank you very much." We would then move on quickly to the next contributor; no undue over-exposure of the name allowed. The ITC were watching us like hawks. Thames Television, the year before, had produced a Telethon for the London area and had made the mistake of handing the microphone over to Robert Maxwell who proceeded to advertise his newspapers.

It was suggested I had a meeting with all the crews involved in *Telethon '88* and that included producers, presenters and reporters from across our region. I stood at the top table in a packed boardroom having been introduced by Emyr Daniel, our programme controller. A sea of faces looked up at me and waited. None of them really had any idea what was expected of them in this 27-hour television marathon. The atmosphere was tense as everyone awaited guidance. I had already thought this meeting through. I kicked off with some magic and jaws dropped. I explained that the *Telethon '88* was all about encouraging the public to do something amusingly unusual for the good of others. Our job was to encourage it and report it. The tricks worked and everyone grasped the idea and worked like Trojans for the entire weekend, making the *Telethon '88* in Wales an unforgettable experience for viewers and fundraisers alike.

We brought in a hypnotist during the night hours but we were not allowed to show the actual act of hypnotism, only the preamble and the person in a trance. Multiply this rule with a hundred others, and you will begin to understand the challenges. As for the actual programme, how do you fill 27 hours of television without sleep, or in our case in Wales, how do you fill ten minutes in every half hour for 27 hours with fund-raising entertainment and be asked by the Network to contribute to their programme as well? The telephone number would go up on screen and viewers would ring in and pledge their amounts of money.

To write of every minute on this television extravaganza would take more than this book, but I will reveal that we survived it with triumphs and disasters and with the generous help of HTV itself, the staff, technicians, the artistes, the fundraisers and, most importantly, those who gave time and money generously towards good causes in Wales. To name all the artistes who helped out over 27 hours would be foolish because there were so many of them but Arfon Haines Davies, Ruth Madoc, Aled Jones, Catherine Zeta Jones, Owen Money, Hywel Gwynfryn, Jean Boht, Bonnie Tyler, Sir Harry Secombe and so many more, in front and behind the camera, gave their time and talent so generously free of charge. There were actors, celebrities and DJs from the Welsh commercial radio stations, even our own presenters and journalists gave of their time. Everyone backed the Telethon; we had Wales covered with outside broadcast units, single electronic camera units with fundraising in north, mid and south Wales. Two studios were operating, one in Cardiff, the other in Mold, and an outside broadcast unit on the promenade in Aberystwyth with Dai Jones and Elinor Jones, and a second one down in Cardiff Bay with presenters, Alan Rustad and Nicola Heywood-Thomas.

We produced another two telethons in 1990 and 1992 – with money for the production becoming less and less. Broadcasters were also battling against 'disability awareness', which was becoming a major issue. LWT was stormed by disabled groups during the 1992 transmission, that is, people fighting for disability rights and banning discrimination towards people with a disability. In Cardiff, all our appeal films, I am pleased to say, gave disabled people a very strong voice and the late Peter Williams, a very close disabled friend of mine, gave us the equality training we needed and helped to protect our transmissions from the interference that might have come our way. The viewing public kept pledging more and more money and performing the most amazing fund-raising stunts, from underwater snooker games, sitting in baths of baked beans, and riding a penny farthing in costume across the Severn Bridge. Even a pensioner coming into the studio with his pension for Telethon, or a small boy arriving with his little money box made me realise the power of television, and that was long before the words 'reality television' had any meaning. Over three telethons, the money collected and distributed through a trust – close on £3 million – would have reached many groups and charities within the principality.

I mention no names in dispatches, other than the late Jane Thomas who could see fund-raising opportunities like the hand in front of her face, and the late programme executive, Emyr Daniel, who asked me to produce the show and set my career on a whirlwind course for the next six or seven years with social action broadcasting. Idwal Symonds, chairman of the HTV Wales board, told me after the 1988 Telethon that we at HTV Wales were favourably comparable to everything he had seen on the ITV Network and that we had every reason to feel proud and rejoice. All ITV Telethon producers from around the country were invited to St James's Palace in London to receive a personal word of thanks from HRH The Prince of Wales and that, for me, was the proudest moment of my life.

***

The telethon was followed by what seemed like a 'reward for good behaviour'. Both Alan Rustad and I set about researching the lives of the three girls we had featured on *Tomorrow's Star Maybe*. Eight years had elapsed. They were no longer schoolgirls, that's for sure. Helen Thorne was engaged to be married and had cast aside any plans she might have had for becoming a star. Suzie was singing to backing tracks in Valley clubs and Catherine Zeta Jones was the star of *42nd Street* in London's West End. The contrast between the three lives could not have been greater, and it was a television programme waiting to be made. Shooting for *West End Girls*, now on video cameras, started in Penarth, where we pushed the engagement party forward to get shots of Helen and her fiancé partying. With Suzie, it was off to the smoke-filled working men's clubs of south Wales and to a West Country seaside resort where she was a support singer in a summer show, and Catherine? Catherine was living the life of a West End theatre star. Interestingly, the story of *42nd Street* is also the Catherine Zeta Jones story. A back-row hoofer in a variety show, the lead performer breaks her ankle and the hoofer is given the opportunity to play the lead with its lethal dance routines and having to appear on stage in every scene, singing, dancing and acting. We filmed Catherine in her London flat, in Covent Garden, and on the Mumbles beach with her friends (half of Swansea turned up!). We shot sequences at her Swansea home and in the Drury Lane Theatre where we recorded at least five segments of the show at a staggering cost. Unquestionably, Catherine Zeta Jones was a celebrity in the making and this was before her appearance on ITV's *Darling Buds of May* and well before her Hollywood career, but Alan Rustad asked her whether she considered herself to be a star. She thought not; she was only known to West End audiences; her career in films had yet to take off, but put that girl in front of the camera lens and she shone like a beacon. It was an indefinable quality, to look so natural, a certain quietness, to under act and not over act, to be herself, natural, talented and beautiful. Emerging from the sea with her friends down on the beach, my cameraman called me over and asked me to look in the viewfinder. Amongst all the figures on the sand, walking up towards the camera, Catherine was undoubtedly the woman the eye rested on.

Alan's interviews with all three girls, the writing and delivery of his commentary was, in my opinion, the most effective piece of television documentary journalism I had ever seen. Simple on the ear, an effective, colourful voice, but narrative written to the point, yet tinged with a slight sadness at what Helen had given up and at the huge effort that Suzie was making to achieve the fame that Catherine had already discovered. Alan told the story so effectively.

We were unhappy with Catherine's 'out words' at the end of the programme. The two other girls had hopes for the future but Catherine had said little to that effect. I rang her at home and called her up to the dubbing theatre on Monday morning. She sat in front of the microphone, looked at the monitor and at the solitary shot of herself on that huge West End stage. She had 20 seconds to speak. She spoke it without fault or hesitation, with all the feeling and thoughts she could muster for her future. She spoke the piece in one take, as Catherine always did.

***

Further to My Application, a documentary on disabled people finding work, was something I had partly come across on the Telethon. I asked Margaret Pritchard whether she would like to present the programme. Her face was familiar on HTV Wales and her involvement with so many Welsh charities made her a strong contender for this documentary as she was genuinely interested in the many issues the programme raised.

Adult Learner of the Year and various other programmes reflecting on the changing face of Wales kept me busy. David Hammond-Williams, our head of religious programmes, asked me if I could produce and direct one programme of the *Highway* series with Sir Harry Secombe in Brecon. With some impressive research by Rosemary Scadden, what a joy it was to work with a man I had listened to on the radio from my early teenage years. He was professional, kind and full of fun, and understood the trappings of television production. All the songs were pre-recorded in a London sound studio and Sir Harry expertly mimed to the music played back to him on location. When once asked by someone whether he would like to be interviewed for *Wales at Six*, he turned round and replied, "What about 'Sharks at Seven'?" Sir Harry always had a large motorised caravan in tow, into which he would warmly invite all his programme guests to relax before facing the camera.

My stint on *Highway* was followed by a live Sunday morning church Eucharist to be transmitted live to the whole country. It was an octagonal-shaped church and difficult to hide the cameras but we managed, just about. Halfway through the preparations, the regular priest was replaced with a new parish priest. Back to the drawing board! Communicants, during my congregational welcome and warm-up, were told to ignore the cameras and enjoy the service. This they did and many of them told me afterwards how much they appreciated the crew holding back on the de-rigging of the equipment until people had finalised their after-service prayers. Praise for the service came from as far afield as Northern Ireland and Scotland.

For Don Llewelyn, a masterly sports producer and documentary maker who had started his own independent television company, I wrote and directed a documentary with Rolf and Anwen Harris, exploring Merthyr Tydfil and uncovering information about Rolf's grandfather, an artist of great merit who had specialized in portraiture and painting still life for the upper classes of Victorian Merthyr. Researched in precise detail by producer and author, Rosemary Scadden, it was a programme of great warmth and charm. It was a joy to shoot and edit, and I literally spent a week choosing the right Victorian music to accompany the pictures. Rolf was a total professional when it came to filming. His appreciation of continuity, lighting, sound and camera angles made him a joy to work with. At no time during the course of work on this project, did any of us believe that, some 25 years later, Rolf Harris would be charged and imprisoned for indecent assault on young people.

Don Llewelyn, a wonderful raconteur in his own right, told me the tale of a certain gentleman who claimed to be responsible for making the cockerel screech at the beginning of the Pathé newsreels by squeezing the bird's goolies. Some bright spark, overhearing the story interjected, "Thank goodness he wasn't working for MGM!"

From all the indications, the 1990s were promising to be as busy as the 1980s.

***

The 1990 Broadcasting Act changed our lives completely. Described by Mrs Thatcher as "the last bastion of restrictive practices", we now entered a new phase of broadcasting when anyone or everyone could claim the right to make programmes. Television was following in the wake of the print industries and the name of Rupert Murdoch was on everyone's lips.

There were staff redundancies every day. The unions were losing their grip. There were terrifying stories in the press about sound recordists claiming unreal expenses at the Zeebrugge ferry disaster. Multiple crews had turned up to interview Margaret Thatcher at 10 Downing Street. There was trouble brewing at TV-am. The IBA (the Independent

Broadcasting Authority – our watchdog) had been abolished and the ITC (Independent Television Commission) became our new regulator, to be abolished in later years and replaced by Ofcom.

The industrial turmoil of the 1980s led to great uncertainty in our workplace in the early 1990s. ITV companies were trimming down, dismantling and restructuring. HTV, like other ITV companies, were having to bid for their franchises to broadcast. With a £21 million price tag for Wales and the West, out went the majority of staff, and in came the accountants with white shirts and red pencils. We had to attend conferences run by business consultants with flipcharts, and we were told that quality programmes could still be made despite much less money and fewer staff. In came stultifying staff reviews where I, as the new head of features, was compelled to interview every member of my staff to see where there was room for savings, improvement in their performance, and increased output. What was the world coming to? We were now all accountable as the once grand figure of 1,500 staff dwindled down to what seemed like a mere handful.

Our audience was now bracketed into social groupings, namely As, Bs, Cs and Ds, and weekly and monthly meetings were held on why some programmes worked and others didn't. It was out with the old and in with the new, and tears were shed by both men and women as their futures became more questionable. Even members of middle management who had done the sackings were being sacked themselves. Redundant technicians queued outside my office door for interviews. Would I be able to use them on future projects?

Redundant directors and producers were offering programme ideas by the crateful and most were starting their own companies, as were cameramen and soundmen, electricians, scene shifters, wardrobe and make-up, vision mixers, editors and designers. Tim, a senior member of staff with his office next to mine in the basement of the studio in Culverhouse Cross, came down one morning with tears welling in his eyes. He had been summoned upstairs to the management: "Who, out of my department, are you taking now?" he asked the boss quite bluntly. There was a pause. "Close the door, Tim, sit down, have a coffee," responded the manager, who looked across at him with a serious look on his face. "It's your turn to go, sunshine." Tim could not believe it. He sat in his office all day afraid to ring home and break the news. He had never thought that his position as the head of a department would go. I was asked myself to sack two members of staff, a highly disagreeable business that left one feeling shaken and uncertain about the future.

A percentage of programmes was now being commissioned out to the new independent sector. No longer would broadcasters have the sole responsibility of manufacturing all their own content. It would make for a richer, more diverse tapestry of programmes and would enable the broadcasting companies to reduce their staffing levels. Channel Four, a publicly owned television body, was commissioning all its programmes from independent producers. S4C had been doing the same in the Welsh language. Both channels had been opened within a day of each other in 1982 and both could commission programmes, not only from the independents but also from the BBC in Wales and HTV in Cardiff. Nothing was more confusing than seeing our studios inhabited by independent companies making programmes for the BBC. What was the world coming to?

The independent sector that had evolved in Wales to make programmes for S4C was having its ranks increased by the number of people leaving HTV Wales hoping to run their own little production companies. Some would succeed brilliantly, others would not. In later years, companies that had enjoyed comparative success were even being absorbed by the larger ones. ITV was changing countrywide, and the unions could do nothing to remedy the situation. For years the regional ITV companies had run unchallenged, but now it was time for takeovers and absorptions by much bigger organisations.

It was during this period of great change in the early 1990s that I put forward my idea for *The Really Helpful Programme*. I had already been told to move my office to something resembling a cupboard in the basement. The new franchise asked for a commitment to social action broadcasting. Paul Starling advised me to absorb as much information on social action issues as possible. He reckoned it would help keep me in work and I had a feeling he was right. Many of my friends and colleagues were to lose their jobs, highly skilled people who were no longer required. For the few of us remaining, draconian cost-cutting measures included the slashing of programme budgets, and living with that put enormous strain on programme makers.

Programmes such as *Telethon* and *Further to My Application* had unwittingly helped my career. From then on I digested everything I could on social action issues. The *Really Helpful Programme*, which went out weekly over five years, covered topics such as charities requiring volunteers, gave a higher profile to medical advice, health and safety advice, financial advice, advice on how to deal with grief, the fear of flying, the fear of heart disease, asthma, and other nasty ailments like flu, appendicitis and the common cold. We discussed legal and consumer problems. We looked at the support available for victims of crime, access in public places for the users of wheelchairs, how to cope with snoring, and how to avoid fire in the home. There were items on benefit and disability allowances and pest phone calls. I submitted my first five programme running orders for *The Really Helpful Programme*. They were accepted and my office moved back up to the second floor.

The Really Helpful Programme ran for five years, won awards and became an astonishing success. It was very much community-based and obviously helped a great many people, as letters from the public and the regulating authority testified. I initially budgeted each programme for approximately £20,000. After a session with a company accountant, that figure was reduced to £2,500, an astonishingly low figure but sacrifices had to be made. There would be no studio with its multi-camera operation – that would cost far too much. There would be no make-up department, presenter Sara Jones would do her own make-up. There would be no production assistant, and we would travel in hired cars to all corners of Wales. All Sara's pieces to camera would be done in the HTV reception area or in an office and we had two days to edit with Simon Johnson, and one morning to dub.

Sara, who asked whether she could come to work with me and proved herself invaluable in so many areas of television production, came from the HTV Wales sports department and was a talented writer, journalist and musician. I was now running the features department, producing and directing my own series and having to convince suspicious and nervous staff that it was possible to make programmes for a fiver and have change left over in your pocket. The trouble was it meant working from early in the morning to last thing at night. The questions I posed at that time, like when do the cuts stop or when can we safely say we are back on terra firma, were never, in my opinion, satisfactorily answered. My suspicions told me that preparation was being made for takeover of the company. If you are lean and solvent, that makes you highly agreeable fodder for the giants of industry.

I became known as the 'studio cat' who was always seen in his office at midnight, head bent low over a mass of paper writing up reports for management, preparing staff appraisals, planning the following day's filming. I once remember working till 9 p.m. on Sunday night and collecting a car from the car park and driving up to Bangor to start filming there the following day. I would be booking into cheap lodgings at 1 a.m. in the morning. A day's filming would follow which involved researching, interviewing, directing and producing, then driving back to Cardiff on the Monday night, checking the post in the office before going home to bed and attending a manager's meeting the following morning, followed by editing and checking on any staff or programme problems that might have arisen whilst I was away up in Bangor.

I had one departmental secretary and a programme secretary, and that was it. We had a team of volunteers to answer phone calls and, Jenny, our helpline manager, who wrote the back-up material to send off to viewers requiring further information. The helpline phones did not stop ringing. They rang incessantly. Viewers out there wanted as much as we could give them. In terms of my own health, I was exhausted, and my home life was non-existent. I was smoking 40 cigarettes a day and beginning to feel drained. Our Welsh board of directors had already gone, and the company was now functioning under new rules and regulations set by the new owner, United News and Media. This scenario was doubtless being repeated in most other regional ITV companies. It was a very sad time and the workload was immense on the few people left behind. In fact, someone on the point of leaving was heard to say, "I pity those of you staying behind." In the sorrow, though, there was still laughter: "Would the last one to leave please put out the lights," someone was heard to mutter.

During the good times, at Christmas, the heads of departments were taken down to the House of Commons to entertain Welsh MPs with some festive cheer. We enjoyed a first-class return train journey from Cardiff to Paddington and an overnight stay at a London hotel. After the event, it was off to a glitzy London restaurant for a slap-up meal. As cutbacks dug deeper, this annual ritual became a picnic basket in the back of a small bus. Gone were the first-class train journeys and the sumptuous meals.

My manager, in my performance review, always wrote glowing things about me but considered my attitude towards management training and audience measurement as lax, and not taken seriously enough. A fair assessment I would say but, in the grand order of things, I had fulfilled, with my colleagues, the Reithian principles of broadcasting, 'to inform, to educate and to entertain'. What more could my audiences ask for? There is no harm in blowing one's own trumpet once in a while. All my programmes had been little crackers! There's that word again! Some maybe not as good as others, but all of them made impartially, in a company I had great respect for, and the viewing audience seemed to enjoy what I was doing. The trouble was, after all my years of struggle and subsequent achievement, I could not take seriously an annual review which reminded me very much of an old school report, and I say that without any form of resentment or bitterness. HTV Wales had provided me with a good life, with a chance to be creative, and in return I had given them total commitment. The television industry, though, had its casualties: separation, divorce and alcoholism were not uncommon and marriage between employees was generally not encouraged.

Prior to a meeting with the ITC in London, my manager asked me to investigate a thing called the 'web' or 'net' that everyone was talking about; there was a chance that people around the London table might know something about it. It transpired that all the companies were developing websites and it was time HTV Wales did the same. It seems strange, looking back, to the time when computers and the 'net' were just talking points and not the business necessity that they are today. I was given the opportunity to develop my department and steer the company towards subtitling, a Teletext service and a website. We had, after all, been the first company to introduce sign language to our news bulletins.

On my cry for more help, Sara and I were given two freelance journalists for the last series of the *Really Helpful Programme*. This was followed with *The Pulse*, a series looking at alternative health issues which was shown on the ITV Network some time later.

I was asked to come up with six half-hour programmes celebrating the 30 years of HTV Wales. I spent eight weekends ransacking the archive which was vast – so many programmes, some of which I could remember from my early days in the company in 1972. Drama, sport, light entertainment, documentary, news, current affairs and religion.

***

From the wonderful opportunities afforded me by Anglia and Grampian Television, even the BBC in Wales, I would suggest that young people entering the industry today are not as honoured with the same privileges and that the world of freelance employment is not as conducive to the permanent, pension-paying existence that I eventually enjoyed. My advice to young people contemplating the media today would be to qualify in something but to look around you. Qualifications are not everything but they denote an interested, enquiring mind. Whether we like it or not, bosses do look for qualification, integrity and personality in the media, and some creative flair would be a bonus. Read books, newspapers and magazines, go to theatres, cinemas, art galleries and museums and ask lots of questions. Never stop asking questions. Listen to the day's news, find out about current issues, listen to the radio and watch television and form an opinion about people, places and events. Be critical of what you see and never stop pushing for what you believe in. Be a blotting paper and absorb all you can. Remember one final thing. If you want something badly enough, you will find the route and if you fall, pick yourself up, brush yourself down and move on.

***

And what of HTV itself? That company which, at the dawn of its franchise, had to win its place in the hearts and minds of the community, had shown its colours against a period of tempestuous change. My programmes were a mere handful against so many other 'classics' produced by my colleagues, all too numerous to mention here. There were such wonderful documentaries and such a broad range of local programmes to suit all tastes. We were constantly under scrutiny by the ITC, now called Ofcom. There were board meetings, departmental meetings, educational panels, religious advisory committees and focus groups, made up of ordinary members of the public who kept an eagle eye on our programmes and were encouraged to comment, be it with criticism or praise. Huw Davies, *quondam* Chief Executive, HTV Wales, said in 2010:

"The focus groups called us 'warm', 'trustworthy', 'homely', 'honest' and 'truthful'. The people we set out to serve seemed to love us quite a bit, and they backed that up by watching HTV more than any other broadcaster in Wales. By the early 1990s, HTV was the biggest producer of programmes on the ITV Network."

***

When I retired from HTV in 1997, revenue was falling, and what was happening to ITV all around the country was calamitous and indicated a decisive victory for those advocating change. But television is a generational thing. Viewing tastes have undoubtedly changed for better or worse, whatever your point of view. Many programmes are now sponsored and suggestions have been made towards permitted product placement. But independent television is a business, and in business one bends with the trend. However, delve beneath the proliferation of television channels today and you will find programmes somewhere with the stamp of quality.

The metamorphosing of the old television set over the years has to be admired, but the quality of the material on view has to take precedence over the technology. Good programmes from Wales with high production values that inform and entertain the audiences have had the stamp of approval from my generation: let that be so for the generations to come.

ITV plc was rebranded in 2004 with the merger of Carlton and Granada and, from 2006 onwards, new logos, digital technology, high definition and the further merging of companies pointed the way forward. What, in my day, had once taken a three-man crew to shoot, can now be done on a mobile telephone. However, the end product might be questionable, lacking in finesse and stability, with inferior sound, lighting and editing and minus the downright stubbornness of a crew who refuse to give up until they get it right. But new technologies and disciplines will undoubtedly win through. I look forward with optimism to a bright new future from the home channel in Wales.

Super charged with all the emotion that only the death of a friend with Aids can bring, I was in the last year of my career when I was asked to produce a 20-minute film for a young gentleman whose partner had died from the disease. Anthony had practically written the script and knew how it was to be delivered. His uncertainty was how to tell the story for television and to make a film with impact and effective enough to be shown on a large screen in front of the City Hall in Cardiff on World Aids day. For me it was an invitation to enter the world of the gay community in Cardiff and feel the tragic pain and remorse of friends and relatives who had seen their loved ones dying from such a global disease. At least 300 people stood and watched the film that cold night, all holding flickering candles, bearing their loss bravely, but celebrating a life and death of someone they had loved who had died through Aids.

I showed the film on *The Really Helpful Programme* the following week and received a very heart-warming letter of thanks from Anthony and his partner's mother. At that very private moment my eyes filled with tears for all the right reasons. At least our programme proved that regional television could be made with and for its local communities, and minorities were always included.

In the rough and tumble world of television, I had anticipated a career finishing around my 40th birthday. The industry had always been run by dynamic, energised young people. I retired in my 57th year but continued working as a freelance director/producer for a short time afterwards. Lady Luck had smiled favourably upon me in realising my ambitions for work in television; she had also given me some lifelong friends and a wonderful family into the bargain.

***

To help bridge my past with what became my future, my swansong, in a melancholy moment, compels me to return to a series I produced in my last year, entitled *Life Begins At...* It was a series of six documentaries looking at older people and their achievements after retirement. I directed one or two episodes, one of which highlighted the life of a man we called Rovi (or Ivor backwards), a north Wales magician who was internationally known as the greatest exponent of close-up magic in the country and in America. I actually managed to get permission, with Rovi's help, to take cameras into the glorious Magic Circle in London – the first time cameras had been allowed on such hallowed ground. Permission came from the great David Berglas, the Grand Master of magic and president of the Magic Circle. After the wrap, Rovi and his fellow magicians took me to a restaurant on the Strand and after the meal and over coffee they continued to mystify me with their own brands of magic. Tricks with coins, tricks with shoe laces, leather wallets, bits of string, thimbles and silk handkerchiefs. I sat there laughing and glowing with pride. I was proud that I was there with them; proud to be experiencing that moment in my life. In my memory, I was back to where I started with my magic on that church hall stage at home near Aberystwyth, only this time, amongst some of the greatest magicians in the country... in that late evening London restaurant... on the Strand.

Whatever happened to...?

WALTER LEWIS, THE magician, now in his early '90s, still entertains his grandchildren in Aberystwyth. The church hall in my village still stands, although now a more comfortable and convenient place. The Wardens Dramatic Society, in which I played my first starring role (!), still entertains local people with impressive summer shows and Christmas pantomimes.

Freshly re-named, The Rose Bruford College of Theatre and Performance in Sidcup and the Royal Welsh College of Music and Drama in Cardiff – also known as the National Conservatoire of Wales – are now internationally known and are vastly expanded as places of learning for artistic and academic achievement.

Welsh film and television director, Geraint Morris (Jack) moved on to the BBC in London where his talent for directing was seen on *The Onedin Line*, *Juliet Bravo* and *Z Cars*. He produced *Softly, Softly* and then helped create the BBC's successful long-running hospital drama, *Casualty*. He later produced the crime series, *Wycliffe*, for HTV and was appointed as their Head of Drama where we met up again after many long years. Sadly, Geraint died of cancer in 1997, leaving his wife, Sian, and two sons.

The old WWN (Wales West and North) Television studios on Western Avenue in Cardiff have long gone and been replaced by the Welsh Joint Education Committee headquarters

My early days in broadcasting were at the BBC television

studios in what had been the Broadway Methodist Chapel in Roath, Cardiff. The administrative offices were in Newport Road, where we planned the productions, and the radio studios and offices were in Park Place. It was a scattered operation until everything was brought together in a purpose-built Broadcasting House in Llandaff, Cardiff, in 1966.

The Welsh National Theatre Company underwent several transformations and closures in an attempt to become permanently housed in a Welsh theatre building of its own in Wales. This was never realised but in 2009 a National Theatre Wales and its Welsh counterpart, Theatr Genedlaethol Cymru, were formed to provide new seasons of plays in different locations throughout the Welsh nation.

The 1,822-seater Odeon cinema in Balham, built in 1938, closed its doors in 1972, opening briefly again under a different banner for the Asian population of Balham, but the final closure came in 1979. The auditorium was demolished to make way for residential flats, but the cinema frontage still remains and now houses retail wine merchants.

Anglia Television, which covered the east of England, has been re-branded as ITV Anglia. It now operates from new premises in Norwich, with additional facilities at Cambridge and Northampton. Its popular flagship news programme continues as *ITV News Anglia.*

Grampian Television in Aberdeen is no more. It was absorbed by Scottish Television in 2006 and provides a daily news service for the north-east of Scotland.

Jim Spankie went on to work for TV-am before starting his own video training service for corporate clients. Calum Kennedy, Bill McCue, Graham Roberts, George Kidd and many others, including my former boss James Buchan, have all passed away and Alan Franchi's memory lives on through his wife, Jane. Eileen Doris Bremner became a talented programme director, as did Hector Stewart for Central Television in Birmingham – both have now retired.

HTV Wales has now been re-branded and become ITV

Wales. They left the Culverhouse Cross studios in 2014 for a new base down in Cardiff Bay.

The Culverhouse Cross studios in Cardiff were once regarded as the most modern in Europe. Handsomely furnished in 1984, there was even money to create a red electronic wave pattern on the carpets stretching down miles of corridors. The equipment for making television programmes was the very best for its time, but someone had forgotten to put windows in the tape editing rooms on the second floor, leaving editors to work in the gloom all day.

Another problem was that the building stood near the Wenvoe television transmitter causing a disturbance to all electronic signals. To help reduce the problem at some additional cost, something called a Faraday Cage was built, a kind of steel mesh, which had to be inserted between the concrete walls around the studios and transmission area.

With such a high profile, royalty were invited to perform the official opening, and a time capsule containing some nuggets of old programmes was buried under the floor to mark the occasion. The canteen was enormous and so was the club, where many a good pint was sunk – a long distance from Grumpy's Grotto in the old Pontcanna studios.

To work the enormous studios and galleries at Culverhouse Cross was like directing a programme from a very smart airport lounge. Talking of which, because of the centre's proximity to Cardiff's international airport, it was not uncommon for passengers to call at our reception to enquire as to the departing time of their flight. The opening night's laser-beam sequence outside the building had air-traffic control in Rhoose ringing us up and telling us to switch it off – it was confusing the in-coming aircraft.

Gone, however, were the cramped little places where we all sat on each others' shoulders in old, antiquated Pontcanna. This was the 'Star Trek: Enterprise', a Captain's log and lounge brimming over with new technology. Office suites fit for a king, dressing rooms, scene docks, wardrobe and make-up rooms, green room with cocktail cabinets and wicker furniture. There was a boardroom and kitchen at roof level to feed the Board members and plans for a cricket pitch and a lake to soothe the troubled brows of programme makers.

This was life during the best of times, all of it funded by commercial enterprise, including the producing and selling of programmes to S4C. We were at the top of the pile in regional television terms and gained significant award-winning coverage for our service to Wales, the West and to the ITV Network.

But this palace of bygone television endeavour is no more and only the memories remain. It was constructed for a time that has long gone and its evanescence brings a tear to the eye. Mind you, many will tell you that not even Culverhouse could surpass the friendship and warmth of the old Pontcanna studios, where we brushed the leaves out of the corridors every autumn and left a saucer of milk in the newsroom every night for the visiting studio cat.

I pay tribute to all my colleagues and friends from the industry over the years, many of whom I shall meet again in future reunions; others have sadly passed away, but one thing we all shared was a profound, dynamic and creative drive to achieve the highest values in television production.

Start the Clock and Cue the Band – A Life in Television
is just one of a whole range of publications from
Y Lolfa. Also available is BBC producer Richard
Lewis's autobiography, *Out of the Valley.* For a full
list of books currently in print, send now for your
free copy of our new full-colour catalogue.
Or simply surf into our website

www.ylolfa.com

for secure on-line ordering.

TALYBONT CEREDIGION CYMRU SY24 5HE
e-mail ylolfa@ylolfa.com
website www.ylolfa.com
phone (01970) 832 304
fax 832 782